YORKSHIRE
THROUGH THE YEARS

YORKSHIRE
through the Years

IAN DEWHIRST

B. T. Batsford Ltd
LONDON & SYDNEY

First published 1975
© Ian Dewhirst 1975
ISBN 0 7134 2882 1
Filmset by
Servis Filmsetting Ltd, Manchester
Printed in Great Britain by
The Anchor Press, Tiptree, Essex
for the publishers
B. T. BATSFORD LTD.,
4 Fitzhardinge Street,
London W1H 0AH and
23 Cross Street,
Brookvale NSW,
2100 Australia

Contents

Acknowledgments

The author and publishers wish to thank the following for permission to use illustrations: Stanley R. Boardman for (70); Cliffe Castle Art Gallery and Museum, Keighley, for (53); C. H. Jones for (34) and Keighley Public Library for (60) and (69).

(13, 23, 24, 37, 40, 44, 47 and 57) are from drawings by N. Whittock in Thomas Allen's *A New and Complete History of the County of York, 1828–31*; British Museum for (6, 8, 17); (1) from Henry Ecroyd Smith's *Reliquiae Isurianae*, 1852; (15) from John Burton's *Monasticon Eboracense*, 1758; (2) from the Rev. Robert Collyer's *Ilkley, Ancient and Modern*, 1885; (27) from the Courtauld Institute of Art; (33) from Francis Drake's *Eboracum* 1736; (29) from Thomas Gent's *History of Ripon*, 1733; (48, 65) from John James's *History of the Worsted Manufacture in England*, 1857; (43) from Thomas Pennant's *A Tour from Alston Moor to Harrowgate, and Brimham Crags*, 1804; (59) the Science Museum; (32) from Ralph Thoresby's *Ducatus Leodiensis* with notes by Thomas Dunham Whitaker, 1816; (16) from John Richard Walbran's *A Guide to Ripon, Studley, Fountains Abbey, Hackfall, and Several Places of Interest*, 1858; (36, 38, 50, 52, and 55) from George Walker's *The Costume of Yorkshire*, 1814; (5, 11, 14, 45, 54, 58) are from the Publisher's collection.

Preface

Yorkshire was Britain's largest county, comprising, according to the Yorkshire Travel Association's definitive count, some 3,923,359 acres—more, by 356,519, than the number of words in the Bible. It boasted another county record in its seven cities ranging from Sheffield, with over 500,000 population, through Leeds, Bradford, Hull, York and Wakefield, to Ripon with its modest 11,000. Yorkshire's parishes numbered 1,568; and its coastline was 117 miles long, with the next highest cliff in England (North Devon's Countisbury easily took the prize) at Boulby. The lengths of all its rivers combined totalled 3,556 miles. Its more recent superlatives included Britain's highest earth-filled dam, Scammonden, and the highest point reached by a motorway, at Windy Hill on the M62. Sadly, at the time of writing, the implementation of the Local Government Act of 1972 is abolishing the old Ridings of the Vikings, and encompassing a massive redistribution of boundaries—though it will take at least another Yorkshire generation or two to speak naturally of their county in the past tense.

The long story of this diverse and sprawling county does not readily lend itself to a comprehensive telling within limited space, and the lives of its people can be glimpsed but impressionistically, age by age. In this task, the author stands indebted to his colleagues at Keighley Public Library, for their obtaining of old and sometimes obscure volumes on his behalf, and for their generous entrusting to him, for the purpose of photographing engravings, of sundry venerable and valuable editions. Further thanks are due to the staffs of Cliffe Castle Art Gallery and Museum, Keighley; Bradford City Libraries; and the individuals and organisations acknowledged for the use of illustrations.

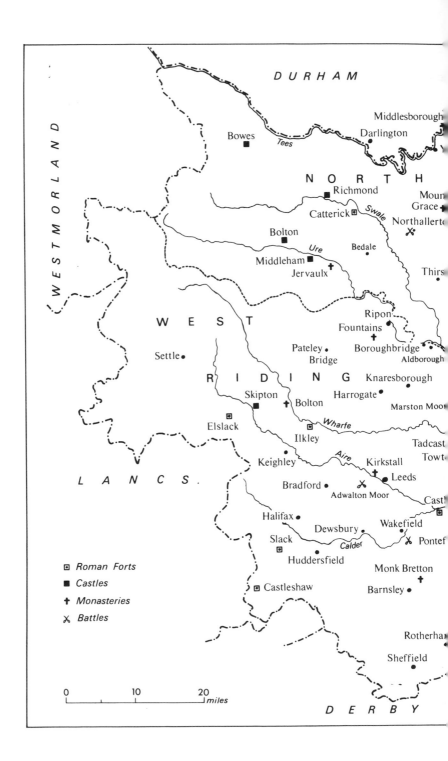

DURHAM

Middlesborough

Darlington

Bowes ■ *Tees*

WESTMORLAND

NORTH

Richmond ■ Moun
Grace

Catterick ⊡ *Swale* Northallert

Bolton ■ *Ure* Bedale ●

Middleham ■

Jervaulx ✝ Thirs

WEST

Ripon ●

Fountains ✝ Boroughbridge ●

Pateley ● Aldborough ●
Bridge

Settle ● RIDING Knaresborough ●

Skipton ■ Harrogate ●

Elslack ⊡ Bolton ✝ Marston Moo

Ilkley ⊡ *Wharfe* Tadcast

Keighley ● *Aire* Kirkstall Towt

LANCS. Bradford ● ✝ Leeds ●
Adwalton Moor ✗ Cast

Halifax ● Dewsbury ● Wakefield ●
Slack ⊡ *Calder* ✗ Pontef
Huddersfield ●

Monk Bretton ✝

Castleshaw ⊡ Barnsley ●

⊡ *Roman Forts*
■ *Castles*
✝ *Monasteries*
✗ *Battles*

Rotherha

Sheffield ●

0   10   20
└────┴────┴────┴────┘ miles

DERBY

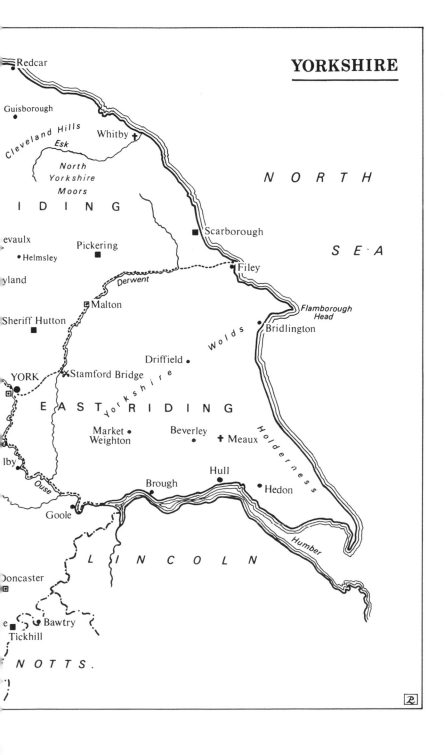

YORKSHIRE

I
Prehistoric and Roman Yorkshire

For millenia, a slowly-sliding sheet of ice, 1000 ft thick and more, had covered all but the highest Pennine hills, melting—about 8000 BC—to leave an empty water-logged landscape strewn with stones, uplands scoured and stripped of soil and vegetation, lowlands muddy with the boulder-clay pulverised, accumulated and deposited by retreating glaciers. Lakes lay everywhere in valleys whose slopes had been ground smooth, their exits blocked with debris.

Before the Ice Age, and in warmer inter-glacial periods, the land had been spectacularly populated by beasts, some few of which, dying in mud or caves, are commemorated by their bones and teeth and tusks. Victoria Cave at Settle, and Kirkdale Cave, near Kirkby Moorside, had been dens of hyenas, whose remains mingled with those of hippopotamus, a straight-tusked elephant, woolly rhinoceros, bear and lion. In Elbolton Cave, near Thorpe, died the Arctic fox and Arctic hare, the reindeer and ptarmigan. Two adult and a young hippopotamus were found bogged down in clay at Armley, Leeds; Raygill quarries at Lothersdale disclosed a slender-nosed rhinoceros, and a lion's tooth; Sewerby, near Bridlington, a bison, a mammoth, a giant deer, a urus or wild ox.

The remote history of a two-legged creature, man, remains largely conjectural. If indeed he ventured to the north of what we now call Britain prior to the end of the Ice Age (and odd bits of stone tool suggest that he did), the glaciers undoubtedly drove him away to warmer climes. But afterwards, as the naked landscape slowly put forth first moss and lichen, then hazel, pine and birch, oak and alder, as lakes silted and rivers cut their courses through moraines, as birds and animals returned, men came walking from the continent across a marshy wilderness that would become the North Sea.

Earliest man was short and stocky, travelling in small bands driven by the necessity of hunting and fishing. Chiefly his first tools and weapons were of stone, chert and especially flint, easily shaped by the chipping off of thin flakes. In the beginning, his, to our eyes, largely wretched existence depended on a multi-purpose pointed tool called a hand-axe; the flakes produced in its manufacture were adapted to scrapers, for cleaning hides; awls, for boring holes in skins; burins, for grooving bones and antlers. Gradually his implements grew more sophisticated: he learned to fix flints into handles and shafts of bone and wood; he shaped and sharpened his axes by grinding rather than chipping.

Remains at Star Carr in the Vale of Pickering offer detailed evidence of the life of one early band, who made their camp on the shores of a mere left by the slow draining away of a great glacial lake. They had built a platform of birch trunks, complete with a landing-stage, though whatever shelter they contrived has not survived. They fished and fowled and hunted elk, roe deer, pig, but principally red deer, eating the venison, fashioning spearheads from the antlers, scrapers from the leg-bones. Their flint axes felled trees, their flint adzes hollowed out a canoe. They ate hazel nuts, made glue out of birch bark, and kept dogs.

Other bands—wandering (though the geography of nations and frontiers was as yet unknown) from northern France—penetrated the less hospitable Pennines. They enjoyed the use of fire and the bow, the sites of their camps and flint-works recorded by their small arrow-heads. Hunters from the south of France bequeathed a few fragments of antler harpoon in Victoria Cave at Settle. But the simple, precarious life of the hunter and gatherer of nuts and berries was gradually superseded by that of the farmer.

The practice of agriculture spread, over many centuries, from the Near East and by way of the Mediterranean and Western Europe, reaching Britain by about 3000 BC. By then, a sinking of the land surface had formed the North Sea and the English Channel, so the advancing race of farmers were capable also of sea-voyages. They heralded, in the Neolithic Revolution of their New Stone Age, as drastic a change as has ever affected mankind. They found a Britain now densely forested, its valleys thick with

1   The Devil's Arrows, near Boroughbridge

oak, so they tended to settle first on higher ground, on heaths
and chalk wolds. Boasting no ploughs, they broke up the ground
with antler hoes or picks, cultivating barley and wheat, domesti-
cating cattle, goats, sheep and pigs, and mastering the craft of
pottery, producing rough brown bowls. Even the rudiments of
specialised craftsmanship and of trade were developed: flint-
mines were dug in southern England; 'factories' at Graig Lwyd in
North Wales and Great Langdale in the Lake District turned
out the polished stone axes indispensable for the clearing of woods,
and these were bartered over a wide area.

The more stable communities of the Neolithic peoples and their
successors of the Megalithic era, relieved of a preoccupation with
mere existence, cultivated an awareness of the spirit. They buried
their dead in long barrows, laid in stone chambers alongside a
central passage, the whole covered with a mound of earth—more
than 20 have been discovered in the East Riding. Sometimes the
remains were cremated. They erected standing stones and circles
of long-lost ceremonial or religious significance, to which later
generations have allotted mythological or more flippant names,

13

like the Devil's Arrows near Boroughbridge, or the Twelve Apostles on Rombalds Moor in the West Riding. The sacred or fertility symbols of a slightly later culture are evident, too, on Rombalds Moor, in the form of numerous boulders chipped with 'cup-and-ring' carvings, their obscure patterns largely made up of dots and circles.

About 2000 BC a new wave of immigrants from the Rhine Valley and the Low Countries carried the use of copper and bronze into Britain. As with their predecessors, we may glean something of their lives from their treatment of their dead, who were now buried, crouched, in round barrows. From their practice of including a beaker of drink to sustain the departed on his last journey, members of this taller race have been called the Beaker Folk. These beakers are of fine pottery, variously bell-shaped or with long or short necks, and decorated with horizontal motifs formed by impressing the clay with combs or cord, twigs or small bones. Other objects buried with the dead indicate that Britain's Bronze Age inhabitants had advanced far from their Stone Age precursors. Their axes were of bronze, and they had bronze knives and daggers, and beads, buckles and buttons of jet. A burial at Kelleythorpe, near Driffield, included arrow-heads and an archer's stone wrist-guard; he had worn a tunic with amber buttons. In time, as cremation became customary, beakers were replaced by cinerary urns and food-vessels.

Trade was developing, with weapons and implements, jet and amber travelling along routes, not only internal, but between Scandinavia and Ireland. In Britain, the age of Bronze, for all its warlike relics, seems to have been relatively peaceful. Not so the age of Iron. During the last several hundred years BC, expanding, questing populations had thrown the continent into a turmoil reflected by the arrival of new groups on the east coast. From Germany came people of the Hallstatt Culture—workers in iron, wielders of sickles and long-swords and spears—who took up a defensive position on Scarborough's Castle Hill; though, less sensationally, the only iron object excavated on the site was a bit of a broken pin.

And from France came aristocratic La Tène warriors, to imprint their clustered round-barrow cemeteries on the Wolds, burying their leaders, male and female, in their two-horse chariots. A woman at Arras, between Market Weighton and Driffield, lay in

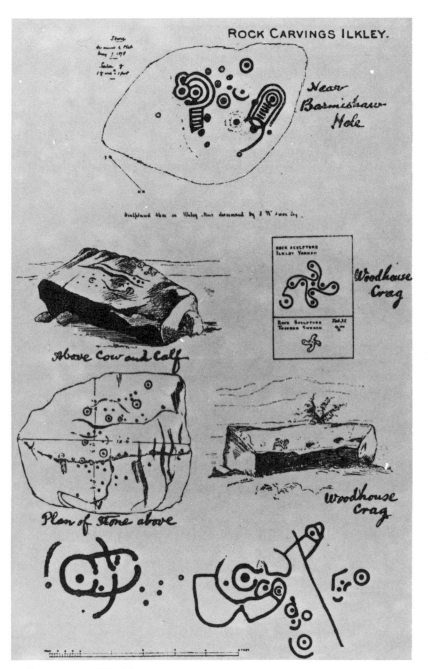

2 *Rock carvings on Ilkley Moor*

her jewellery of glass beads, gold and amber rings, bronze brooches and armlets. Two hundred barrows in a misnamed site at Danes' Graves. north of Driffield, suggest a cult insofar as bodies had been buried along with pigs and legs of pork. Harness and accoutrements found at Stanwick St John, near Richmond, show an artistic use of metal and enamel, with designs inspired by horses' heads. Eventually, such flamboyant newcomers conquered—or rather, perhaps, imposed their influence upon—a native population leading a hardy peasant life. The climate had deteriorated, about 500 BC, growing colder and wetter, so the Celtic farmers tended, like their New Stone Age predecessors, towards better-drained limestone pastures. The typical family group of the period occupied a circular hut of boughs and skins above a gravel bank, surrounded by their oblong irregular horse and stock enclosures walled with stones or turf. In the north of England they seem to have subscribed to a mysterious cult involving the carving of oval-eyed, slit-mouthed stone heads now unearthed alike near natural springs and on virgin moorland. They can have been little match against more sophisticated military neighbours.

So, in Britain, the last centuries before the birth of Christ witnessed a confused, obscure inter-tribal fighting, with hill-tops taking on a new significance as places of refuge and defence. Out of what must have been considerable struggles and stratagems (Danes' Dyke, near Bridlington, fortified a five-mile-square peninsula by means of a ditch 60 feet wide and a bank 18 feet high) appeared a tribal confederacy, the Brigantes, conjecturally originating from the Lake Constance region whence they took their name, from the town of Brigenz. For 8,000 years, the country between the Humber and the Tees, and from the Pennines to the east coast, had received and assimilated different continental races, different cultures, different skills; but only with the Brigantes, holding loose dominion from the Rivers Mersey and Trent northwards across the Scottish borders, does an approximate territorial concept emerge. Perhaps, we might say, though Brigantia included more than Yorkshire, the Brigantes were, in part, the first Yorkshiremen.

Then in 43 AD the Romans invaded Britain. Brigantia, the Roman historian Tacitus had heard, was 'the most populous state in the whole province' of Britain. To be sure, most of its population consisted of poor small farmers, yet it was minting, albeit crudely, a gold coinage decorated with wreaths and symbolic chariots and inscribed with the names of its rulers: Volisios, Dumnocoveros, Cartimandua—a coinage which, through having been found sprinkled among Roman Republican money, suggests some pre-invasion trading. The Brigantes' larger settlements were forming the basis for towns which, being subsequently occupied by Roman forts, have come down to us by Romanised names. Camoludunum (Almondbury, near Huddersfield) was possibly their capital; and they had also founded, among others, Vinnovium (Binchester, near Bishop Auckland), Isurium (Aldborough), Olicana (Ilkley), Cataractonium (Catterick), and Eboracum (York).

But events were to prove that the Brigantes were not a unified people. In 51 AD, having subjugated the south, the Romans attacked and defeated the Silurian tribesmen of the Welsh borders, whose leader, Caratacus, sought refuge with Cartimandua, queen of the Brigantes—who promptly handed him over in chains to the Romans. Paraded in Rome, Caratacus's dignity so impressed the Emperor Claudius that he was liberated; Cartimandua's Roman sympathies wreaked more serious consequences.

She had married Venutius, a sub-chief hostile to the Romans: now a Brigantian civil war broke out, with Roman troops called in to bolster Cartimandua's shaky authority and quell Venutius's supporters. For some years the queen spent Roman subsidies in dissipation—it was in the Roman interests to keep a friendly Brigantia between themselves and the Scots tribes—and not until 69 AD did the relationship of this dramatic and regrettably obscure couple end, when Cartimandua divorced Venutius to marry his armour-bearer! Once more civil war erupted, and this time Cartimandua had to flee to her allies for sanctuary, whilst Venutius prepared to resist a Roman invasion.

Says Tacitus, tantalisingly brief, 'the battles were many and sometimes sanguinary, but the greater part of the Brigantian territory was either annexed or devastated'. To this period probably belong the Brigantian fortifications on top of Ingleborough, an inhospitable if defensive position, as every walker who has toiled up this most popular West Riding peak would agree: the whole 16-acre summit was walled and dotted with circular huts on stone foundations. Venutius's main defences,

3 *Statue of a Roman soldier unearthed at York*

however, were constructed at Stanwick, north of Richmond. Set in a rolling landscape, Stanwick enjoyed no obvious military significance, but boasted a good water supply in what is now quaintly termed the Mary Wild Beck. Here Venutius chose to erect a complex system of ditches and ramparts more than 20 feet high in places, enclosing an area of over 700 acres and necessarily employing considerable Brigantian forces. The works were never, in fact, completed, succumbing to the assault of a Roman army under governor of Britain Petilius Cerialis in 74 AD—one relic retrieved from the ditch near an entrance was a decapitated skull, much slashed about the eyes.

The fall of Stanwick saw the end of effective Brigantian resistance to the Romans, and a few years later the governor Agricola began consolidating the occupation of the north in earnest, bisecting the map with roads strategically watched by forts. The landscape was still heavily forested, its marshy lowlands restricting the scope of movement and settlement, so that the Romans were largely compelled to adapt existing sites and routes; yet it is the road system they perfected which provides our first basic geography of the area that would become Yorkshire.

Northward from their fortresses at Chester and Lincoln came two main highways, one on either side of the Pennines: the former by way of Manchester, Ribchester and Low Borrow Bridge to Carlisle; the latter crossing the Humber to Brough, thence swinging north-west to York, Aldborough and Catterick, then up to Corbridge in Northumberland. Another road out of Lincoln led north through Doncaster and Castleford, meeting, near Tadcaster, an east–west route from Ribchester through Elslack and Ilkley to York and on towards the coast. Other cross-country roads went from Manchester to York by way of Castleshaw and Slack; and from north of Catterick through Bowes to join the Chester–Carlisle road. Another, north-eastward from Manchester, crossed the Ribchester–York road at Ilkley and continued to Aldborough. This great military network effectively enmeshed and subdued the native population.

Roman roads—mileposted and carefully documented in guides issued to commanders and officials—were kept secure by patrols from forts erected at strategic intervals: first simple ramparts of earth and timber replaced, as time passed, by more durable stone structures, till streets laid out among barracks and stables, stores, commandants' quarters, and sometimes even bath-houses, made up the Romans' typical rectangular forts. Eventually, too, many were adjoined by civilian settlements formed by soldiers' families. The Ninth Legion, which was posted to York, had seen distinguished service in Spain; but the task of policing the smaller forts along the roads devolved upon auxiliary troops recruited from among conquered European peoples. And bleak, in north British winters, their duties must have seemed to them, for these were not the bronzed breast-plated figures of legend, but workaday men in boots, hoods and mufflers, with tunics and breeches of leather, who in their off-duty hours indulged in ball-games and cock-fighting, played dice and draughts, and worshipped a diversity of gods borrowed from the far-flung provinces of their Empire.

York, or Eboracum, made an obvious focal point, a road centre ideally situated for a legionary fortress, commanding as it did a natural crossing of the Ouse and equally accessible to the level east and the hilly west. The river was navigable up to that point, facilitating supplies, and York steadily grew from clay fort to handsome stone headquarters town. Malton (Derventio) controlled the Parisi—a tribe originating from the Seine valley who had settled in East Yorkshire—and Aldborough (Isurium) became a civilian centre; but it was York that Emperors visited and governors made their residence. Here the Emperor Septimius Severus died in 211 AD, after some 'black sacrificial animals' had been carelessly allowed to follow him 'to the very threshold of the imperial abode'—an ill omen—and York citizens were treated to the flamboyant ritual of his funeral pyre, his ashes alone being shipped to Rome in an alabaster vase. At York, too, Constantius Chlorus died a century later, his son, the future Constantine the Great, being proclaimed there ruler of the western Empire: his cremation sported a showmanlike detail in the releasing of an eagle, 'the multitude following its flight with shouts and prayers, supposing that therewith the emperor was mounted into heaven'. York has bequeathed many relics of the Romans, but none more moving than their altars and tombstones:

'To the spirits of the departed. Lucius Baebius Crescens, from Augusta Vindelicorum, soldier of the Sixth Legion Victorious, Loyal and Faithful, 43 years of age and of 23 years service' . . .

'Corellia Optata, 13 years old. I, the pitiable father of an innocent

4 *Roman tombstone at York*

daughter, caught by cheating hope, lament her final end' . . . 'Lucius Duccius Rufinus, son of Lucius, of the Voltinian tribe, from Vienne, a standard-bearer of the Ninth Legion, 28 years old. He is laid here' . . .

The lot of the Brigantian fighting-men following their defeat at Stanwick is partly conjectural. Some may have provided a captive labour force when the Romans exploited the lead deposits of Swaledale and Greenhow, as they probably would slave at road-building. But northern revolt kept flaring up afresh, even after the completion of Hadrian's Wall had penned back the Scottish tribes. Sporadically, in the second and third centuries, forts were burned, and rebuilt. Near Keighley, beside the Manchester–Ilkley road, Romans had occasion to bury a copper chest described on its resurrection in 1775 as 'perhaps the noblest discovery ever made in Roman Britain', containing a calculated 100 lbs weight of coins and a silver image; but Georgian locals, eager to satisfy the antiquarians and convert their finds to contemporary cash, dispersed the hoard as effectively as if it had been buried afresh. The matter remains a mystery—like another unanswered question of the Roman occupation, namely the fate of the Ninth Legion, which about 122 AD was replaced at York by the Sixth, from Germany.

But gradually some at least of the tribesfolk integrated with the Romans, who were to remain in Britain for three and a half centuries. On the one hand, veteran soldiers retiring from service stayed in Britain, living with their families outside the forts; in the third century, one such settlement near York was proclaimed a colonia, or chartered community for Roman citizens. And on the other hand, the more aristocratic Brigantes cultivated a taste for the benefits of Roman civilisation. Aldborough, or Isurium Brigantum, near Boroughbridge, on an earlier site as evidenced by the Devil's Arrows, became the Brigantian tribal capital. 'The soil of the locality,' rather disagreeably commented one historian in 1852, 'has been so greatly enriched, at the expense of the reliques of art, as seldom, if ever, to require the application of manure; it is mostly black in colour, and abounds in fused and decomposed organic matter'. The stone walls of Isurium were used by later generations of builders, and for cobbling the streets of Boroughbridge; but surviving remains are eloquent of Romano-Brigantian culture. This city, of possibly some 3,000 inhabitants,

5 *Roman mosaic pavement at Rudston*

had boasted baths and shops, a basilica or judgement hall, houses with sculptures, tesselated floors, and wall paintings imitating marble, a pottery, and possibly an amphitheatre and race-course. For centuries, spades have turned up spoons, dice, rings and beads, coins, combs, thimbles and brooches, the artifacts of a sophisticated society. Petuaria (Brough-on-Humber) similarly formed a capital for the Parisi of East Yorkshire—this town boasted one of only four Roman stage theatres discovered in Britain—whilst Romanised villa farms, producing corn, centred on Malton, which also developed glass and pottery industries.

Towards the end of the third century, this consolidating Romano-British culture was threatened from a new quarter in the shape of coastal raids by pirates from across the North Sea. At first cautious and sporadic, these steadily escalated until, in conjunction with attacks by the Irish, Picts and Scots from the west and north of Hadrian's Wall, they posed a serious menace, and in 367 were repulsed only at expensive cost in lives and morale. Hence, the Romans created a commander, Count of the Saxon Shore, responsible for coastal defence. Malton was made a military base, a fleet posted in the Humber, and the east coast watched by a chain of signal stations at Saltburn, Kettleness, Ravenscar, Scarborough and Filey. These stone-walled positions mounted catapults, but their chief feature was a wooden semaphore tower for signalling movements at sea. They were probably garrisoned by local militia, since by the fourth century the Brigantes and Parisi were so far Romanised as to be enlisted in their own defence.

In the end, events on the continent, where the Roman Empire was in process of declining and falling, drained Britain of soldiers. The Wall was abandoned in 383, whilst early the following century remaining Romans withdrew to the south. The ruins of Yorkshire signal stations offer a glimpse of what followed: at Huntcliff, near Saltburn, the bones of men, women, children and dogs were found thrown together in the well; at Kettleness, the skeletons of a man and a dog lay locked, the dog's head on the man's throat. It was a savage and symbolic prelude to six centuries and more of invasion.

FURTHER READING

General
Edward Hailstone: *Portraits of Yorkshire Worthies*, 2 volumes, 1869.
Marie Hartley and Joan Ingilby: *The Yorkshire Dales*, 1963.
Marie Hartley and Joan Ingilby: *Yorkshire Portraits*, 1961.
E. F. Lincoln: *The Heritage of Yorkshire*, 1967.
John Mayhall, compiler: *The Annals of Yorkshire*, c. 1866.
William Page, editor: *The Victoria History of the County of York*, 1907–23.
A. C. Price: *The County of the White Rose*, 1915.
Arthur Raistrick: *The Pennine Dales*, 1968.
William Arthur Shuffrey: *Some Craven Worthies*, 1903.
W. E. Tate and F. B. Singleton: *A History of Yorkshire*, 1965.
George Walker: *The Costume of Yorkshire*, 1814.

Chapter 1
E. T. Cowling: *Rombalds Way: a Prehistory of Mid-Wharfedale*, 1946.
Frank and Harriet Wragg Elgee: *The Archaeology of Yorkshire*, 1933.
Amédée Forestier: *The Roman Soldier*, 1928.
Sidney Jackson: *Celtic and Other Stone Heads*, 1973.
Gordon Home: *Roman York*, 1924
Alan King: *Early Pennine Settlement: a Field Study*, 1970.
I. H. Longworth: *Yorkshire* (Regional Archaeologies), 1965.
F. R. Pearson: *Roman Yorkshire*, 1936.
Arthur Raistrick: *Ice Age in Yorkshire*, 1968.
Arthur Raistrick *Prehistoric Yorkshire*, 1964
Arthur Raistrick: *The Romans in Yorkshire*, 1965.
Royal Commission on Historical Monuments: *An Inventory of the Historical Monuments in the City of York: Volume I: Eboracum: Roman York*, 1962
Henry Ecroyd Smith: *Reliquiae Isurianae: the Remains of the Roman Isurium*, 1852.

2
The Dark Ages

The departure of the Roman legions left northern England in a parlous state, devoid of troops, its people clustering round towns suddenly grown quiet, or still hardily farming in scattered communities little altered by Roman rule; whilst Picts and Scots and Irish pillaged from the north and west, and pirates sailed in from the east. Truly, these were the Dark Ages; though perhaps the Venerable Bede gave too lurid a description of hapless Britons sinking under the barbarians' onslaught: 'Leaving the cities and the wall they fly, and they are scattered. The enemy followeth upon them, hasteth to slay more cruelly than he did before. For even as the lambs of the wild beasts, so were the wretched citizens mangled of their enemies: whereupon being driven out of their own homes and possessions they falleth a robbing and spoiling one the other of them, to stay the peril of hunger that threatened them'.

The coastal invaders were coming from Baltic regions, where a gradual earth movement had caused the sinking of coasts and valleys with subsequent loss of land, over-population and migration. The Angles were from South Denmark, the Saxons from North Germany and Holland, the Jutes from Jutland: the dominant group to reach the north of England became the Anglians. *The Anglo-Saxon Chronicle*, possibly almost contemporary, suggests that, in 443, Britons employed Anglians as mercenaries against their more traditional foes, first asking the Romans 'for help against the Picts; but they had none, because they were themselves warring against Attila, king of the Huns. And then they sent to the Angles, and entreated the like of the ethelings of the Angles'.

Steadily the incursions of Angles penetrated inland by means of rivers, until their expeditions took on the nature of an immigration. Serious clashes may indeed have been rare, since they tended to avoid existing towns, settling on the slopes of the Wolds and more tentatively into the Vale of York. A pagan culture, their cemeteries, where both cinerary urns and skeletons lie in rows, have yielded a harvest of food-vessels, beads, combs, knives, spindle-whorls, spears and shield-bosses—and incidentally suggest the briefest hiatus between Romans and Angles, since the latter wore Roman coins as ornaments. By the middle of the seventh century, grave-relics grow scarcer: the Anglians were being Christianised.

The early Angles had moulded the country east of the Pennines and north of the Humber into a kingdom called Deira, whilst a Celtic community retained awhile the forest of Elmet in the present Leeds region. North of the Tees, the Angles also founded the kingdom of Bernicia. Then Ethelric, son of a king of Bernicia, married a princess of Deira and thereby united both provinces into the Anglian Kingdom of Northumbria. Edwin, who succeeded to the throne in 617, annexed Elmet and politically married Ethelburga, a Kentish princess and a Christian. When Ethelburga travelled north in 625, the Roman missionary Bishop Paulinus came with her. Paulinus—'a man,' Bede tells us, 'of excellent understanding, sitting oftentimes by himself alone for a great space, in much silence of outward voice'—emerges as one of the most determined figures in a period which of necessity demanded strong characters. Pope Gregory had sent him to Britain in 601 to assist Archbishop Augustine of Canterbury. His time was not ripe for another quarter-century; but once his short-lived opportunity arose he grasped it, trudging about the Kingdom of Northumbria doggedly preaching though not, to begin with, converting.

Edwin was eventually persuaded to the faith by the coincidental dramas of an attempted assassination and his wife in labour. 'When,' Bede relates, 'the king in the presence of the bishop Paulinus gave thanks to his gods for the birth of his daughter, the bishop contrariwise began to give thanks to the Lord Christ, and to add furthermore that he hath obtained by his prayers of Christ, that the queen might bring forth her child safely and without grievous pain'. Edwin's resulting conversion was celebrated by the building of the first humble wooden church on the

27

guinem innocentem condempnabit.

6 *Ploughing, Old English style*

site of York Minster. His erstwhile pagan chief priest, meanwhile, helped destroy his own temple! Thereafter, Paulinus found his converts, baptising many in the River Swale above Catterick.

Yet Christianity was not destined to enjoy a smooth acceptance. In 633—even as he was beginning 'a basilica of stone greater and more magnificent' around York's wooden church—Edwin was killed in battle at Hatfield against the combined forces of Penda of Mercia, or the Midlands, and Cadwallon of Wales. Once more the land reverted to obscure pagan warfare; slaughter ran rife in the north; Paulinus and Queen Ethelburga returned sadly to Kent. Indeed, the real hero of Augustine's mission to the North may well have been James, Paulinus's deacon, a man 'extraordinarily skilful in singing', who, remaining at his post after his master's flight, kept a flicker of faith alight. Yet it was left, in these confused and blood-soaked times, to a dedicated trio of kings called Oswald, Oswin and Oswy to stamp Christianity more firmly among the people of Northumbria.

Oswald, reared in the monastery of Iona, raised a cross before his army near Hexham and led them to the defeat and slaying of Cadwallon; to be himself slain by Penda eight years later. Of the gentler Oswin, King of Deira, it was said 'the nation is not worthy of such a ruler'—he was murdered by his cousin, Oswald's younger brother Oswy, who thereafter atoned for his deed by killing Penda —then a hale 79-year-old—'and the Mercians,' the *Anglo-Saxon Chronicle* significantly adds, 'became Christians'. Oswald and Oswin were canonised.

The Christianity prevalent in the Kingdom of Northumbria by the middle of the seventh century, had originated from Ireland, as established by Saint Columba on the Scottish island of Iona.

Here Oswald had lived in exile, in a monastery composed of mud and wattle buildings surrounded by an earth rampart; and, when he won Northumbria in 634, he summoned, not a Roman missionary from the south, but a Celtic bishop from Iona. The one first sent, incidentally, soon returned with the tale that the people were too rough and barbarous; but a more determined Aidan set up his headquarters on Lindisfarne, whence he proceeded to evangelise the North of England. Yorkshire's first monasteries were founded at Gilling, near Richmond, in 642, at Ripon in 660, and at Lastingham and Hackness. The most important was built at Whitby in 657, under Abbess Hilda, a relative of the late King Edwin. These early monasteries were humble collections of wattle huts with stone foundations, enclosed within a defensive wall; that at Whitby seems to have included a farm.

The Celtic and Roman Churches followed different traditions. The Celts set little store by organisation or wealth, preferring a simple, direct contact with the people by means of travelling missionaries who earned their food and shelter along the road with a prayer or a blessing; the Romans believed in the discipline of dioceses. Celtic monks shaved their hair in front and let it grow long at the back; Romans adopted the circular tonsure on top of

7 *Making an enclosure of wattle*

29

their heads. They had alternate methods of calculating the date of Easter. Their differences were debated in 664 at the Synod of Whitby, when the Roman pattern was adopted in preference to the Celtic, and whereby, whatever Christianity in the North might have lost in evangelical fervour, it gained in the culture and order of the Roman faith.

The visible result of this emergence of Roman Christianity was a flowering of art and literature. Bishop Wilfrid, appointed to York in 669, had visited Europe and acquired a taste for architecture and ceremony; now he looked critically at Paulinus's neglected church, its roof leaking, windows empty, walls damp, serving 'only for the nesting place of birds'. Accordingly, he 'strengthened the masonry, raised the roof, and when it was raised, protected it from injury by storms with leaden sheets. In the windows light came through linen cloths or a fretted slab'. It was at York, in the following century, that the scholar Alcuin presided over the cathedral school of learning and a fine library—reputedly the best in Europe—before accepting Charlemagne's invitation to help initiate a revival of continental culture. 'How sweet was life,' he would urbanely reminisce, 'while we sat quietly among the rolls of the wise, among abundance of books, among the judgment of the revered Fathers'.

Epitomising the studious life of the period, another churchman, the Venerable Bede, spent nearly 60 quiet years in the monasteries at Monkwearmouth and Jarrow, which had been richly stocked with books. 'I wholly applied myself to the study of Scripture,' he related, 'and amid the observance of monastic discipline, and the daily care of singing in the church, I always took delight in learning, teaching and writing'. His Latin *Ecclesiastical History* (translated into English by Alfred the Great) presents an invaluable record of the events and personalities of seven centuries. Again, in Hilda's monastery on the cliffs at Whitby, a cowherd Caedmon, ashamed because he could not take his turn singing at supper, crept out to receive inspiration and compose the first English poem:

Now we must praise the Guardian of Heaven,
the might of God and his mind,
the work of the Father of Glory, since he hath performed each wonder,
the eternal Lord, the beginning.

He first shaped for the children of the earth
the heavens as their roof, the holy Creator . . .

This direct religious feeling found more concrete expression in the tall, wheel-headed Anglian crosses, originally marking the preaching places of itinerant priests, remnants of which survive— carved with mixed Christian and mythological motifs—in Yorkshire churchyards like Masham and Ilkley.

Then began a yet fiercer invasion, first from Denmark and later from Norway. The Vikings may have derived their convenience name either from *vik*, meaning a creek or bay, or from *vikja*, loosely translated as 'one who makes a long journey away from home': both being applicable to this pagan seafaring race. Their graceful longships, prows decorated with animal heads, masts and coloured sails developed to a high technical degree, were superior to any vessels their contemporaries could launch against them. Masters in battle primarily of the axe and the two-edged iron sword, buoyed up by sagas extolling the courage and ruthlessness, stoicism and fidelity of their heroes, the Vikings posed a formidable threat to Christian peoples, who had good cause to pray, 'Save us, O God, from the violence of the Northmen'.

They first raided England in 787, killing a sheriff who 'knew not who they were'. 793 brought storms and famine which the Kingdom of Northumbria interpreted—accurately, as it happened—as 'dire forwarnings' of worse to come. Vikings destroyed Lindisfarne monastery, and looted Jarrow the following year. Commented the gentle Alcuin: 'Never before in the 350 years that we and our forefathers have dwelt in this fair land has such a horror appeared in Britain as this that we have just suffered from the heathen'.

But the serious Danish invasion of the Northumbrian province of Deira did not come till 867, when an army fresh from a conquest of East Anglia crossed the Humber and bloodily captured York. The Danes 'knocked down all the boys, young and old men they met with in the city, and cut their throats,' one old account conjures up the terrors of that time. 'Matrons and virgins were ravished at pleasure. The husband and wife either dead or dying, were tossed together; the infant, snatched from its mother's breast, was carried to the threshold, and there left butchered at its parents' door to make the general outcry more hideous.' In a spate of plundering, the monasteries at Whitby and Hackness and Lastingham were sacked; although, after a decade of battles and treaties, the invaders followed the now-familiar pattern and began to settle. In 876, the *Anglo-Saxon Chronicle* records, they 'apportioned the lands of Northumbria, and they thenceforth continued ploughing and tilling them'.

The Viking Kingdom of York has left its mark on modern Yorkshire. It can be seen in the Old Norse and Danish place-names sprinkled across the Dales and the Vale of York, more noticeably on the moors and hillsides they preferred to make their homes: in the suffixes '-by' (a farmstead or village) and '-thorp' (an outlying farm); in 'force' for waterfall, 'ing' for meadow, 'carr' for marsh. York itself, the 'Eoforwik' of the Anglians, became the Viking 'Jorvik', and the city retains a strong Scandinavian influence in its use of 'gate' for street: Goodramgate was 'Guthrum's street', Skeldergate (skjaldari gata) the street of the shield-maker, Haymongergate (heimangari gata) the street of the hay-merchant. The many Viking relics unearthed at York have included rings and beads, tools and whetstones, draughtsmen carved in bone, and silver coins minted there.

8   Old English warriors—including a chief and his shield bearer

It was the Danes who divided Yorkshire into its thridings, or thirds, which formed the basis for the Ridings, each administrative unit further split into Wapentakes, so called from the 'weapon-grasping' or 'weapon-shaking' by which representatives signified their assent to decisions reached at public assemblies. Wapentakes took their names from the meeting-places of their courts; hence, Skyrack derives from the 'Shire Oak' at Headingley, Ewcross from a cross, Agbrigg from a bridge. The Danes, too, abhorred capital punishment, decreeing 'gentle' measures against their wrongdoers—though, since these included the cutting off of ears, noses, lips and hands, the pulling out of eyes, and scalping, they were of dubious 'benefit to the people'.

Yorkshire's now variegated peoples were blending in a largely agricultural way of life. Angles and Danes tended to farm the plains and valleys, Norsemen to run sheep and cattle on the hills. The hamlets of the former presented a cluster of houses and small crofts about an open space that would eventually become the village green, surrounded in turn by common fields rotating between wheat, barley and fallow. Ploughs were laboriously drawn by oxen, whilst lean, long-haired pigs foraging half-wild in the still plentiful woodlands provided a staple diet. The homesteads of the hill-settlers, on the other hand, were of necessity dotted about the lonely fells.

The influx of the pagan Danes and Norse, with their monastic depredations, had shaken but had not subdued the progress of a determined Northumbrian Christianity—the monks of Lindisfarne carried the bones of their St Cuthbert hither and thither for years before laying them to rest at Durham—and eventually it was the invaders who were themselves Christianised. Politically, however, the Vikings brought two to three centuries of violence and upheaval to England. Their period chronicles a confused melée of war and pillage and sudden death. The predictably bloody collapse of the Viking Kingdom of York in 954, and Northumbria's change of status to an earldom under King Eadred of Wessex, gave no respite to a catalogue of strife, the closing and typical chapter of which has become notorious through its being so closely pursued by larger events.

Edward the Confessor, King of England, died at the beginning of 1066 and was succeeded by Harold, whose brother Tostig had proved so ruthless a governor of Northumbria that he had been exiled. On Harold's accession, Tostig allied with Harald Hardrada, King of Norway, whose fleet sailed up the Humber and whose army captured York. The English under Harold made a forced march northwards, meeting and crushing the Norwegians at Stamford Bridge, killing both Hardrada and Tostig. This Yorkshire battle—savage even by the no-quarter standards of its day, for the English 'hotly smote' the enemy fleeing to their ships, till 'some were drowned, and some also burned; and thus in divers ways they perished'—is famous for its graphic tale of the lone Norwegian who held the bridge: 'an Englishman aimed at him with a javelin, but it availed nothing; and then came another under the bridge, and pierced him terribly inwards under the coat of mail'.

But Tostig and Hardrada were not the only invaders that autumn. Within days, Duke William of Normandy, harbouring an obscure claim to the English throne, had landed on the south coast. Harold turned his weary army southwards again to meet him and to fall, on 14 October 1066, at the battle of Hastings.

FURTHER READING

Chapter 2
Bede: *Historical Works*, with an English Translation by J. E. King, 2 volumes, 1930.
Johannes Brøndsted: *The Vikings*, 1960.
B. E. Dodd and T. C. Heritage: *The Early Christians in Britain*, 1966.
Leighton Houghton: *In the Steps of the Anglo-Saxons*, 1948.
D. P. Kirby: *The Making of Early England*, 1967.
Charles Plummer and J. Earle, editors: *The Anglo-Saxon Chronicle*, 1952.
F. S. Popham, editor: *A History of Christianity in Yorkshire*, 1954.
Arthur Raistrick: *Vikings, Angles and Danes in Yorkshire*, 1965.
A. H. Smith: *The Place-Names of the East Riding of Yorkshire and York*, 1937.
A. H. Smith: *The Place-Names of the North Riding of Yorkshire*, 1928.
A. H. Smith: *The Place-Names of the West Riding of Yorkshire*. 8 volumes, 1961–63.

3
Norman and Medieval Yorkshire

Norman rule would bring a measure of discipline and stability to England, welding its rival kingdoms and variegated peoples into the semblance of one state. For Yorkshire, however, the era dawned in fire and blood.

William consolidated his victory at Hastings with a speedy conquest of the south, and on Christmas Day was crowned in Westminster Abbey. Marching north in 1068, he built a castle at York—which was promptly besieged by local rebels and had to be relieved and supported by a second castle. But the summer of 1069 brought a more serious threat to William's authority, when a strong Danish attack by way of the Humber met with English support. The Norman garrison at York was slaughtered, the city plundered by both sides. 'When the king heard of this,' the *Anglo-Saxon Chronicle* tersely relates, 'he went northward with all the troops he could collect, and laid waste all the shire.' His march against York cut a swathe of devastation across the landscape, his short sweeping campaign being followed by his ruthless 'Harrying of the North.' Putrefying corpses littered the roadsides; famine and pestilence raged: the results were still apparent two decades later in the Domesday Book, which records extensive tracts of Yorkshire as 'waste'.

Local historians have long stood indebted to King William's Domesday Survey of 1086. He was not, of course, considering the historians when he held 'deep speech with his Witan' or court, and initiated this 'record from which there was no appeal'; rather was he concerned with the extent of his realm, the ownership of its lands and resources, and the amount of taxes it might be expected to yield. Nevertheless, his clerks and questioners, riding

·xxj· TERRA GISLEBERTI DE GAND.

ESKEDING

In HVNDEMANEBI· hb Carle· xxuii· car' tre
ad gld· tra e ad xiii· car'. Nc Gislebt' de gand.
he ibi· iiii· car' 7 uiii· uill 7 ui· bord· hntes· iiii· car'.
Ibi pbr 7 eccla 7 ptu· i· leu lg· 7 dimid lat'.

In ead uilla hb Chilbt· i· car' tre ad gld· tra ad dim c
Gislebt' he 7 Wast' e· T·R·E· ualt· iiii· sol.

In RISTORP· e Bereuu hui· co· iiii· car' tre ad gld·
tra ad· iii car'. Ibi he Gislebt'· u· uill 7 ii· bord cu· ii· c
Ad hoc co panet soca h. Muston. Scolfstona.
Hotemanebi. Simul ad gld· xiiii· car' tre· tra
ad· uii· car'. Ibi he Gislebt'· xui· uill· 7 iiii· bord·
hntes· iiii· car'.

In NEVTON Bereu hui· co· uii· car' tre ad gld·
tra· ad· iiii· car'. Tot hundemanebi· iii· leu lg· 7 ii· lat
T·R·E· ualt xii· lib· m· lx· sol

9 *Extract from the Domesday Survey relating to the East Riding*

out among the shires and villages and wrestling with strange tongues, compiled the first great detailed description of England. County boundaries were not altogether defined in 1086, and Yorkshire still included parts of Lancashire, Westmorland and Cumberland. For this admittedly larger area the Domesday Survey catalogues some 794 places as 'waste', where lay land once cultivated and now neglected, as compared with 68 in Derbyshire and 54 in Nottinghamshire. Probably not all this depredation can be blamed on the Normans, but also on the Danes and the general uncertainties of the times. For the rest, the Yorkshire of 1086 emerges as a predominantly rural society: the city of York then numbered possibly a thousand houses, and the Domesday Book records only four other boroughs: Dadsley and Tanshelf (that is, Tickhill and Pontefract) in the West Riding, Bridlington and Pocklington in the East.

The shire's estates were measured by the carucate, which represented approximately 120 acres or the amount of land that could be tilled in one year using one plough and a team of eight oxen; naturally, this was not a fixed unit, being likely to vary according to the nature of the ground, and the West Riding carucates especially might have been on the smaller side. A basically peasant population was composed largely of sokemen or small land-holders and, lower down the social ladder, bordars and villeins, who were poorer but possibly free. Domesday makes no mention of the serfs who, presumably in Yorkshire as in other counties, provided the lowest class of workers. The Survey does, however, credit Yorkshire with 133 priests and six iron-workers; also with 18 fisheries, 92 mills and 162 churches.

Theoretically after 1066 the whole of England passed into William's possession, and he rewarded his followers with slices of his new realm. To his half-brother Count Robert of Mortain went some 215 parcels of Yorkshire, many in Cleveland and the north-east of the county; to Count Alan the Red, of Brittany, the great tract of the Honour of Richmond. Ilbert de Lacy acquired Pontefract and much of Airedale; Roger de Busli, the Honour of Tickhill in the south; William de Percy, whose descendants would become the powerful Earls of Northumberland, parts of the Dales and the coast; Robert de Romille, Craven and upper Wharfedale. . . . Hence, the Norman Conquest grafted a foreign aristocracy on to an English structure whose

37

10   *The keep of Richmond Castle*

nobility had died in the battles of 1066 or the subsequent rebellions, had gone into exile or had been dispossessed. By William's death in 1087, only an estimated eight per cent of English land remained under its pre-Conquest owners, by which time perhaps 200,000 Normans and French had settled amongst a native population fallen to a million and a half. The feudal pattern which emerged under William the Conqueror would set the seal on Yorkshire history throughout the Middle Ages.

The county was apportioned amongst some 29 Norman tenants-in-chief, who held their nominally Crown estates in return for their military support; they in turn could sub-let their lands to lesser tenants on similar conditions. The basis of society came therefore to rest on the estate or manor, a lord's influence depending on the number and extent of manors he held, and a peasant's lot, be he freeman or bonded, being governed by the manor to which he was attached. The lord of a manor might well be an absentee, leaving administration and the necessary raising of revenues in the hands of his steward, so that country life took on a more businesslike aspect than hitherto. The peasant's life became increasingly regulated: in addition to his quota of physical labour for his lord, he must—if, as was often the case, he worked any scrap of a holding for himself—grind his corn at his lord's mill, pen his sheep in his lord's fold, even pay for his lord's permission for his daughter to marry. His hovel remained for centuries the rudest shelter against the elements, and his livestock perhaps shared it with him; his bed of straw and rushes on the damp earth stiffened his limbs with arthritis, broke his health with rheumatism.

Yet the age found its folk-hero, in Robin Hood, whose outlaw band in Lincoln green, robbing the rich to give to the poor, are popularly associated with Sherwood Forest but feature equally in Yorkshire ballads, tales and place-names. This bold figure, slaying the King's deer and flouting Norman authority, must have provided an apt escapism for the peasantry who comprised four-fifths of England's population. Beyond the romanticism, too, lay a solid reality, as the forests, still covering a third of the land, harboured many wretched, shivering men skulking beyond reach of the barons' laws. A reputed gravestone near Huddersfield was inscribed with a quaint rendition of the local dialect:

> *Hear, undernead dis latil stean,*
> *Laiz Robert, Earl of Huntington;*
> *Nea arcir vir as him sa geud,*
> *An pipl kauld him Robin Heud;*
> *Sick utlauz as hi, an iz men,*
> *Vil Inglande nivr si agen.*

Power in Norman England was symbolised by the castle. The first were of the simple type called 'motte-and-bailey', whereby a flat-topped mound of earth (the motte) was separated by a ditch from a lower enclosure (the bailey), the whole being surrounded by a ditch and stockade; a wooden tower on the motte serving as the main defence in the event of the bailey being overrun. The

11 *Bolton Castle in Wensleydale*

motte of William the Conqueror's second York castle of 1069 survives as Clifford's Tower; it was thrown up in eight days, which suggests the employment of considerable native forced-labour. The great stone castles came more than a century later, under Henry II, as rectangular keeps replaced the motte and curtain walls defended the bailey.

Each Norman lord, building his stronghold in a landscape dependent, for its sense of geography, on roads, tended to choose the best strategic site available to him, so that Yorkshire acquired a slightly fortuitous defensive system of castles. Bowes guarded the road from York to Carlisle, Pickering that from Malton to the north, Skipton the Aire Gap through the Pennines, whilst York's castles—never entrusted to the loyalty of henchmen but retained by the Crown—stood at the centre of the county's old and still valid Roman road network. Knaresborough dominated the River Nidd, Richmond the Swale, Scarborough occupied a dominant coastal position. Life in Norman castles was harsh, their earlier buildings usually of timber; and, if a chapel and private chambers for the lord were customary features, the main hurly-burly centred upon the communal great hall.

The Norman Conquest brought a continental flavour to English

Christianity. There was, to be sure, no sudden or drastic change; rather, a gradual replacement of native bishops and abbots by Normans and Frenchmen with motives political as well as religious, who, like William's castle-building barons, formed part of a system for stabilising the country. These newcomers, fresh from a Europe clothed already with a magnificent 'white robe of churches', looked askance at the small Saxon chapels with their solid but clumsy walls and tiny windows. Ripon Cathedral and York Minster had indeed existed for centuries, but the great monuments now demanding of our awe are of Norman inspiration —though the latter would be 400 years in the building, its new works rising gradually outside the old, its worshippers for generations threading their way among masons', carpenters' and glaziers' tackle. The flame of English monasticism, too, was burning low by the late eleventh century; the turbulent times had cast small bands of monks adrift searching for a retreat, and now it came within the means of the Norman aristocracy to grant lands for the support of the stone abbeys and monasteries which replaced earlier and architecturally modest foundations, as a variety of new religious orders superseded the Celtic.

The Benedictines, the oldest monastic order, were known as the Black Monks by virtue of their black habits. Scholars and teachers,

12   York Minster

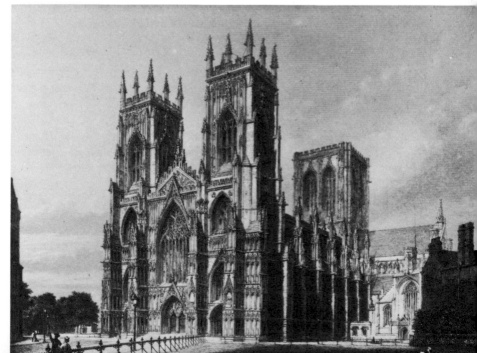

some of their early houses—Goathland, Grosmont, Hackness, Middlesbrough—have bequeathed no trace; pirates drove them from Whitby and Lastingham; Count Alan of Brittany founded their wealthy York St Mary's Abbey. The Cluniacs, fonder of ceremony than the Benedictines, settled at Pontefract and Monk Bretton. The Augustinians—the Black Canons because of their black cassocks—numbered Bolton, Bridlington, Guisborough and Nostell amongst their Yorkshire foundations. The Carthusians, clad in white cassocks and black cloaks, their faces cowled, each silent in his cell, would be represented (albeit not for another three centuries) by Hull and Mount Grace Priories. But ultimately greatest of all in Yorkshire were the White Monks or the Cistercians, more austere than their fellow-orders, 'glorying in their poverty'; not scholars, but believers in a simple life of hard physical work. To the Cistercians we owe the stately grey splendours of Fountains Abbey, of Rievaulx and Jervaulx, Kirkstall and Byland.

To the Cistercians, too, is Yorkshire indebted on more practical grounds. One feature of early monasticism was its economic activity, as monks who were also land-holders exploited the agricultural and mineral potential of their estates. The Cistercians were especially industrious, surrounding their abbeys with farms and managing their outlying lands from granges. Fountains Abbey, for example, developed granges specialising in iron-working, lead-smelting, horse-breeding and sheep-farming. Often the wasted estates they were granted seemed fit only for sheep: their Latin chronicles nicely convey the Rievaulx landscape on their arrival in 1131—*in loco horroris et vastae solitudinis*. A short-lived foundation at Barnoldswick struggled awhile with 'the inclemency of the air and the ceaseless trouble of rain' before moving to Kirkstall; whilst Fountains on its foundation was described as 'a place uninhabited for all the centuries back, thick set with thorns, lying between the slopes of mountains and among rocks jutting out on both sides: fit rather to be the lair of wild beasts than the home of human beings'. Notwithstanding which, within three decades the house was swarming 'like a hive of bees' with 140 monks and 600 lay brothers. 'Our food is scanty, our garments rough, our drink is from the stream,' one of them wrote, 'under our tired limbs there is but a hard mat; when sleep is sweetest we must rise at a bell's bidding.'

13 *Fountains Abbey cellarium*

The Cistercian order had originated in wool-producing Burgundy; so it was natural that they should turn their main energies to their extensive Pennine and Cleveland sheep-walks. Kilnsey in Wharfedale became each year the bawling, teeming centre for their shearing. Steadily the Cistercians grew rich on wool; their houses were beautified by means of wool; the Fountains Abbey cellarium was built as a wool warehouse (at its peak Fountains boasted 18,000 sheep). Latin was used as a business tongue in common with the continent. In conjunction with an immigration of Flemish weavers during the twelfth and thirteenth centuries, they founded Yorkshire's wool trade. A surviving merchant's list of 1280 to 1315 contracts for 3,291 sacks of wool from the whole of England: 1,446 of which came from the Cistercians.

Under the influence of wool, York prospered on its navigable Ouse, as dealers or 'wolmongers' set up an export centre for the North. Less than a century after Hastings, the Weavers' Guild of York had a charter whereby 'no one except them shall make any cloths dyed or striped in the whole of Yorkshire, except the men of York unless it be others of the same occupation in Beverley, Thirsk, Malton, Kirkby, Scarborough and other royal boroughs'. For this privilege the York guild paid the Exchequer £10 a year, coming second only to London, whose weavers paid £12; those

43

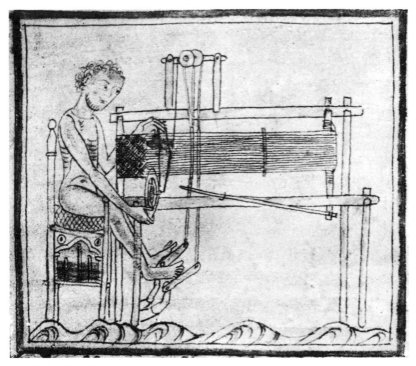

14 Medieval weaving

of Lincoln, Winchester and Oxford combined paid only £6. By
the thirteenth century Beverley and Hull had also emerged as wool
centres.

None of this occurred against a peaceful background, for Scots
invaders were replacing coastal raiders as the chief threat to the
stability of northern England, and Yorkshire's vulnerability
explains why its nobles were allowed to grow powerful. The
Honour of Richmond, comprising no less than 242 manors from
the Ure to the Tees, formed an unusually large block of land
awarded to one family—the Dukes of Brittany—and the great
names to achieve prominence, the Percies and the Nevilles, the
Cliffords and the Mowbrays, would owe their rise in part to this
need for defence against the Scots. For centuries, harvesters would
work with their weapons close at hand in case of sudden attack;
parish priests would lead their contingents to the muster; monks
would occasionally abandon their houses to take refuge under

castle walls. Yet, for all Yorkshire's castles, the fortunes of Scot and Sassenach swayed back and forth. Near Northallerton in 1138, old Archbishop Thurstan of York took out an army against King David of Scotland, blessing his troops on the battlefield before a Host mounted on a ship's mast on a waggon, above the banners of St Peter of York, St Cuthbert of Durham, St Wilfrid of Ripon, and St John of Beverley: the resulting English victory was named the Battle of the Standard. On the other hand, an English defeat at Bannockburn in 1314 opened the gates afresh for Scottish raids; whilst the White Field of Myton on the Swale, in 1319, claimed 300 slain from among the fighting English clergy of the age.

Nor did violence spring only from external forces. William the Conqueror, recognising the commercial genius of the Jews, had encouraged their settlement in England, and a thriving, though unpopular, community had established itself at York. The intrusion of a number of Jews into Richard I's coronation at Westminster sparked off a pogrom which spread to the provinces, and in 1190 the Jews of York, harrassed by the city's more unruly residents, took refuge with their families and possessions in what old chroniclers call the Castle, but what was more likely the keep of Clifford's Tower, from which they barred the governor who had admitted them for their safety. There they were besieged by an infuriated mob exhorted by a friar, whose braining by a large stone dropped from the battlements sealed the Jews' death-warrants. Many of the men killed their wives and children, set fire to their stronghold and committed suicide; the rest were massacred and their goods looted when they perforce admitted their attackers into the burning Tower. The dead were estimated at a doubtless highly exaggerated 2,000, and records of the Jews' financial transactions were fired in the Minster nave.

A picture of Medieval life both monastic and agricultural survives in the Compotus or household book of Bolton Priory between 1290 and 1325, 'a folio of a thousand pages, very fairly written'—according to antiquarian Thomas Dunham Whitaker at the turn of the eighteenth century—in a rather daunting 'kind of patois, consisting of Byzantine Greek, Italian, old French, and Latinised English'. The impression it gives is far removed from meditation and the seclusion of cloistered lives. Bolton Priory, on the banks of the River Wharfe, stood then in a heavily wooded

45

landscape, where wolves still prowled. An Augustinian house, its
15 to 18 canons were supplemented by lay brothers, gentlemen
retainers, and a motley crowd of serfs and free servants which
swung its population to about 200 souls.

Life in a religious community was, in effect, busy and boisterous,
much concerned with practicalities. In 1301, Bolton Priory
counted 713 horned cattle, 2,193 sheep, 95 pigs and 91 goats. Its
mills and granges spread far; extra help at harvest-time included
over 1,000 haymakers at a wage of twopence a day. It worked a
lead-mine, collected tolls from Embsay fair, and kept a forge
going; ran a bercary or shepherd's lodge at Malham, and another
at Nussay on the edge of Knaresborough Forest. The Priory
estates bustled with cooks, carpenters and herdsmen, smiths and
bakers and brewers. The Compotus supplies all the details: we
know that Malham bercary was roofed with shingles, Nussay
thatched with ling; that men guarding the livestock were armed
with bows and arrows; that sheep were rubbed with oil and fat
to kill vermin; that reapers were given gloves, and shearers aprons.
We even know their rustic names—John de Lambhird, Adam
Blunder, Tom Noght, Whirle the Carter and Botchcollock the
Cowper, Richard Drunken, Adam the Stockman and Simon
Paunche. Outdoor appetites accounted, in a single year, for the
slaughtering of 64 oxen, 35 cows, a steer, 140 sheep and 69 pigs,
the consumption of huge quantities of wheaten bread and oatmeal
pottage, the malting of 636 quarters of oats for ale, and the pur-

46

chase of 1,800 gallons of wine. The Priory oven was so big that once, after the Dissolution, it sheltered a flock of 60 sheep. Serfs dragged the river and ponds with nets, and fish was brought from Lincolnshire. Women milked the sheep; butter was made from ewes' milk, and, in 1310, 147 stones of cheese ('I have tasted this preparation,' commented the painstaking Dr Whitaker five centuries later, 'and found it extremely disgusting').

The Augustinians had moved a long way indeed from their vow of poverty. Their habits were of fine cloth costing three shillings a yard—the wages of free servants ranged from ten to three shillings a year; two horses, by comparison, were sold for more than £9. Hoods were lined with expensive furs, budge, white hare and lambs' skins. The Prior, who journeyed extensively, to York and even to Rome, had 20 servants and enjoyed sumptuous rooms and a feather-bed. Travellers sampling monastic hospitality slept on mats in the guests' hall; but patrons were entertained on a lavish scale, dining on salmon, eels, partridges and, choicest of all, heron. When Archbishop Melton of York visited Bolton Priory, a phenomenal £23 19s 5d was spent on his retinue and his pack of hounds.

The torch of learning was kept alight, though perhaps it did not burn over-brightly at Bolton: at any rate, they bought three books in 40 years, and a picture of St Cuthbert, and paid 16 shillings for 'gold and colours', and for illuminating and binding a missal. *The Book of Sentences*, by Peter Lombard, cost 30 shillings—the price of a score of sheep. The monastic vow of obedience seems also to have worn thin: one William de Appelton was caught poaching and refused to reform, despite a penance which included scourging, confinement to the Priory, and a simple fare of bread, beer and vegetables on Fridays! He was finally packed off for correction to Thurgarton Priory, in exchange for a wayward Thurgarton canon who, 'taking delight in debates and envyings, constantly stirs up strifes, quarrels, and backbitings among his brethren'. A lay brother, contrary to the rule of poverty, hid his life's savings of 100 shillings.

The troubles of the outside world constantly intruded. In 1300 the Priory's ox-drawn wains were pressed into service carrying the baggage of an English army against the Scots (they had difficulty getting them back), and some of their livestock helped victual a later expedition. After Bannockburn the canons fled several times

47

to the shelter of Skipton Castle, carrying such stock and moveables as they could. Once the Prior refugeed into 'Blackburnshire', and the canons dispersed to other Augustinian houses. Their granges were overrun; in 1319, the year of Myton, they kept no accounts, because of the Scots.

Meanwhile, urban life was developing. A great many Yorkshire towns owe their growth to the nucleus formed by a Norman or Medieval castle, church or religious house, or to the granting of a market charter. As a source of revenue, the right to hold a weekly market and annual fair was prized by the feudal lord: 'Charter Roll 33, Edward 1: For Henry de Keighley, Know ye that we have granted and by this Our Charter have confirmed to our beloved and faithful Henry de Keighley, that he and his heirs may have one market on every seventh day, being a Wednesday, at his manor of Keighley in the county of York, and one fair therein every year lasting three days namely:—on the eve on the day and on the day following of St Simon and St Jude, unless

16   Monastic doodles: sketches from Fountains Abbey. The central figure represents a knight against whom the inmates waged a lawsuit

that market and that fair be to the injury of neighbouring markets and neighbouring fairs . . .' Temporary stalls were in time replaced by permanent shops; trade attracted growing populations.

By the fourteenth century, York numbered more than 13,000 citizens, spilling outside the protection of the walls which had reinforced its earlier earth ramparts, a city including 40 churches, chapels, guild halls, hospitals, schools, prisons and inns. From the lantern-tower of All Saints, Pavement, shone a lamp to guide benighted travellers through forests where wolves still prowled. Its streets were crooked and narrow, undrained and indifferently cobbled; market-places and cloisters provided its principal open spaces. Houses ranged from palaces to hovels, the wealthier of stone and timber: rooms were small, ill-lit and unventilated. Butchers slaughtered livestock in the midst of habitations, and rubbish was thrown into the streets—'Go beneath the surface in the York streets,' one future historian would remark, 'and you will find that the most solid part is a vast accumulation of bones' thrown out of the houses. Wooden shops crammed across the Ouse bridge; single-masted ships with high prows and deep holds clustered at the Ouse quays. Beverley stood almost as high as York, its 38 trade guilds regulated by a complex of ordinances— bakers were not to employ Scotsmen, saddlers were not to make reins. Hull's role as a port increased with its trade in wool and cloth. The Calder Valley became dotted with fulling-mills washing the grease out of rough wool. The Poll Tax returns of 1379 reveal developing towns at Pontefract and Doncaster, Sheffield, Selby, Wakefield, Bradford . . . in effect, the pattern of Yorkshire's towns was emerging.

Populations did not grow painlessly, in ages largely innocent of sanitation and fresh water, when rush-strewn floors gathered dirt and germs for months at a stretch, when harvests were uncertain and the poor depended on an unbalanced diet of rye-bread, beans, salted pork and even acorns. Medical attention, such as it was, came through the well-meant but limited ministrations of monks; hospitals were attached to religious houses but, though fairly numerous in centres like York and Pontefract, were intended rather as a refuge for the destitute and incurable than for the treatment of the sick: many were simply leper-colonies. At Ripon, the hospitals of St John the Baptist and St Mary

Magdalene merely catered for 'poor clerks', some 'four or five of whom were to have soup daily and beds at night', and provided 'all poor persons seeking alms with soup twice a week'; the smaller Maison de Dieu kept 'two common beds for every lone travelling man that hath noe spending'. St Leonard's Hospital at York, mindful of the wretched poor, gave away 33 dinners and 14 gallons of beer every Sunday, supplied a weekly loaf to prisoners in the Castle, and distributed 256 herrings a week. For the most part, however, medicine was a hopeless—sometimes actively harmful—mixture of astrology and superstition. Epidemics were an ever-present dread. The Black Death of 1349 killed a third of England's population, and one estimate puts Yorkshire's toll as high as half—one victim was Richard Rolle, poet and mystic, author of *The Pricke of Conscience* and called the Hermit of Hampole, near Doncaster. More than half the clergy died: at Meaux Abbey, ten survivors out of 50 had to promote their sub-cellarer to abbot. 'Crops,' writes the historian of Meaux, 'lay rotted on the ground, stock had perished, for there had been no one to gather in the harvest, no one to water or feed the animals; the future was gloomy, no one remained to begin the autumn ploughing.' This situation, indeed, hastened the disintegration of the old feudal system, as surviving peasants now, by their very scarcity, given the advantage over their lords and bailiffs, were able to commute their compulsory labours for payment, whilst hired workers cultivated the manor lands.

Nevertheless, Medieval life enjoyed its lighter side. Comic stone faces grinning down from cathedral walls perpetuate the drolleries of anonymous workers; craftsmen carved wooden misericords with homely scenes of daily activity and folklore: a fox running off with a goose in his mouth, chased by a woman with a distaff; a pair of pigs playing bagpipes . . . Popular entertainment coupled with basic religious instruction is glimpsed in the mystery plays of York and Wakefield. At York, every Corpus Christi Day, at half past four of a June morning, the first of 57 movable stages would set out from Pageant Green on a tour of the city, each manned by a trade guild and each enacting a short play at perhaps a dozen points, so that onlookers at any one spot during the day could see the entire cycle covering the stories of Adam and Eve and the life of Christ: the coopers presented Adam's fall from grace, the tile-thatchers Joseph and Mary, the

17　A Mystery Play

18　Humour . . . pigs dancing to bagpipes, from a misericord at Ripon Cathedral

painters the Crucifixion, and so on. The Wakefield cycle similarly offered the Nativity and the Resurrection, with the Old Testament episodes of Noah and Jacob. Yet mystery plays were more than simple dramatisations of well-worn tales; they were enlivened by the detail, humour and reality of their times. Hence, a character in the Wakefield Second Shepherds' Play opens with a speech coloured, we may imagine, by his own experience:

> *Lord, but this weather is cold, and I am ill wrapped,*
> *My hands in frost's hold, so long have I napped;*
> *My legs they fold, my fingers are chapped,*
> *It is not as of old, for I am lapped*
> *In sorrow . . .*

and the play draws ribald fun from the bickerings of a husband and wife, and the swaddling of a sheep in babies' clothes.

But ultimately Yorkshire's Medieval heritage survives rather in its architecture, dwarfing the human concerns of those who lived against a backcloth slowly evolving in style from Norman through Transitional to Early English, to Decorated and Perpendicular: in the rounded arch of Adel Church doorway and the soaring white towers of Beverley Minster; the glorious ruins of the rich Cistercian abbeys and the small austere cells of Carthusian Mount Grace Priory; in Conisborough's great cylindrical keep and Skipton's mighty gate-towers. Man-placed stones still counterpoint the broad-acred landscape, though the powers and politics of the men themselves were doomed.

FURTHER READING

Chapter 3
Adolphus Ballard: *The Domesday Inquest*, 1906.
Battle and District Historical Society: *The Norman Conquest: its Setting and Impact*, 1966.
H. C. Darby and I. S. Maxwell: *The Domesday Geography of Northern England*, 1962.
David C. Douglas: *William the Conqueror: the Norman Impact upon England*, 1964.
J. S. Fletcher: *The Cistercians in Yorkshire*, 1919.

Herbert Heaton: *The Yorkshire Woollen and Worsted Industries, from the Earliest Times up to the Industrial Revolution*, 1965.

J. L. Illingworth: *Yorkshire's Ruined Castles*, 1938.

K. A. MacMahon: *Beverley*, 1973.

W. R. Mitchell: *The Haunts of Robin Hood*, 1970.

A. Leslie Mollett: *York's Golden Fleece*, 1962.

Rev. J. S. Purvis: *The York Cycle of Mystery Plays*, 1951.

Arthur Raistrick: *The Role of the Yorkshire Cistercian Monasteries in the History of the Wool Trade in England*, 1953.

Ripon Civic Society: *Ripon: Some Aspects of its History*, 1972.

Martial Rose: *The Wakefield Mystery Plays*, 1961.

O. G. Tonkeieff: *Life in Norman England*, 1966.

Thomas Dunham Whitaker: *The History and Antiquities of the Deanery of Craven in the County of York*, 1805.

Kenneth Wilson: *Abbeys of Yorkshire: a Tourist's Guide*, 1969.

4
The Wars of the Roses and the Reformation

There are inherent dangers in a policy of rewarding service with lands and power, and sanctioning the indiscriminate building of castles. William the Conqueror had recognised this, ensuring, for the most part, that his nobles' estates did not lie in too sizeable a block—Robert of Mortain's 800 manors, for example, were split across 20 counties—but strongpoints had been essential in the consolidation of the Conquest; whereas some of his successors, weaker or less astute, found themselves embarrassed by his legacy. Notably the reign of Stephen had witnessed 12 terrible years of baronial anarchy and led to Henry II's attempts to limit the strength of feudal lords. In the North, however, the threat of Scottish invasion had ensured a still-powerful nobility which continued, long after the border had grown quieter, in the emergence of great families like the Percies and Nevilles, the Cliffords and Mowbrays. Their tenants and retainers were virtually private armies. Given an explosive situation, they could influence the succession to the very throne of the realm.

Trouble, indeed, had been brewing since 1400, when Richard II had been murdered and succeeded by his cousin Henry IV, son of John of Gaunt, Duke of Lancaster and Edward III's fourth son. The House of Lancaster ruled through Henry V to Henry VI, but the latter's bouts of insanity gave countenance to the rival claims of Richard, Duke of York, descended from Edward III's third son. In 1455 England lapsed into 30 years of intermittent civil war.

The Wars of the Roses bore no relation whatever to the popular vague notion of 'Yorkshire fighting Lancashire'; the white and red roses were not yet county symbols, merely the personal badges of the royal houses of the Dukes of York and Lancaster. Ironically, during a struggle wherein the nobility sided with one or the other contestant, the majority of Yorkshire's great families supported the Lancastrians: the mighty Percies, headed by the Earl of Northumberland, with estates stretching from the Border to the East Riding; the Cliffords of Skipton, the Scropes of Castle Bolton, the Roos of Helmsley, the Dacres, the Greystokes. . . . Only the Mowbrays of Thirsk joined the Nevilles of Middleham and Sheriff Hutton in the Yorkist cause. The power and privileges of the feudal aristocracy went down forever in a long-drawn flurry of battle and sudden death.

In a preliminary skirmish and Yorkist victory at St Albans in 1455, Northumberland and Clifford were killed. The Duke of York's capture of King Henry at Northampton in 1460 was the signal for Yorkshire's Lancastrian forces to muster against him, and, marching north to meet them, he died in battle at Wakefield, his army surrounded 'like unto fish in a net'. It was here that Lord Clifford earned his grisly notoriety and nickname 'The Butcher' by reputedly stabbing York's young son with the words, 'By God's blood, thy father slew mine, and so will I do to thee and all thy kin', and setting up the Duke's head, wearing a paper crown, over the Micklegate Bar at York. An elated Lancastrian march on London dissipated itself in rape and pillage and, retreating, paid terrible retribution on Palm Sunday of 1461, at the hands of York's elder son, now proclaimed Edward iv.

The battle of Towton, near Tadcaster, saw a bloody decimation of Yorkshire's Medieval nobility. 'By mutual agreement,' relates an old account, 'no quarter was to be given by either side, and no prisoners were to be taken.' A snowstorm blew squarely into the faces of the Lancastrians, their arrows fell short, and savage hand-to-hand fighting lasted, it is extravagantly said, for ten hours. The swollen Cock Beck ran red with blood allegedly for two days after the battle; and when the Lancastrians fled in confusion, men weighted with armour drowned in it, their bodies providing a bridge for their comrades. 'Butcher' Clifford caught a headless arrow in the throat at nearby Ferrybridge. Lord Dacre was shot when he improvidently took off his helmet to drink a cup of wine. The Earl of Northumberland was carried away to die of his wounds at York. Lord Scrope was badly hurt. At least, one prisoner was taken 'when they were weary of killing' — the Earl of

19 *Mickelgate Bar, York*

Devonshire—though he was not allowed to live for long. Contemporary chroniclers, over-awed at the scale of the slaughter, put the toll at an exaggerated 38,000 dead, who were buried in 'certaine deepe trenches overgrown with brushes and briers containinge 19 yards in breadth and 32 yards in length'. Four centuries later, ploughmen and archaeologists were still turning up skulls and bones, though Victorian souvenir-hunters had managed to exterminate the dwarf roses, 'white with a red spot in the centre of each of their petals', which grew on the field.

The immediate effects of Towton were the replacing of Yorkist with Lancastrian heads above Micklegate Bar, and the confiscation of Lancastrian estates. The Percy lands and titles were given to the Yorkist Nevilles; Lord Roos turned to piracy; the 'Butcher's' son, young Henry Clifford, gained a future place in Wordsworth's poetry and his own more pleasing nickname, the 'Shepherd Lord', by being allegedly brought up as a simple shepherd. An uneasy truce broke in 1470, when Richard Neville, Earl of Warwick, 'the Kingmaker', changed sides, briefly reinstated poor mad Henry VI, and died in battle against his erstwhile allies at Barnet the following year. A further victory at Tewkesbury, and the execution of Henry, placed the Yorkists yet more firmly in control. Young Richard of Gloucester, son of the Duke of York, married his cousin Anne Neville, the Kingmaker's daughter, and came to govern the troubled North from the Nevilles' Wensleydale fortress at Middleham, where he had spent much of his boyhood.

Richard of Gloucester remains a controversial figure for historians who hotly debate both the existence or otherwise of his notorious crook-back, and the extent of his implication in the murder of his nephews—the Princes in the Tower—by which, following the death of Edward IV in 1483, he became King Richard III. Be that as it may, he knew how to win the respect of a sullen North. His only son was born and died at Middleham, where Richard secured a charter for the village to hold two annual fairs. 'He came very rarely to court,' one contemporary noted. 'He kept himself within his lands and set out to acquire the loyalty of his people through favours and justice.' He stabilised the Scottish border; became a patron of Yorkshire churches; set up a council of advisers which diplomatically included Lancastrian supporters, and which administered justice for the poor as well as the rich; and even established a series of posting stations, for royal messengers between the North and London, which anticipated our postal system by centuries. Despite the weightier burdens of state, he recognised the details from which spring popular discontents, and took pains to remove obstructive fishgarths—fixed nets to catch salmon—from the Rivers Ouse, Aire and Wharfe. His relations with York were especially friendly. His visits to this bustling city of churches and guilds were greeted with ceremonial gifts of fish and wine, and his opinion was sought as to the choice of Lord Mayor. He attended the mystery plays, and in 1477 he and his wife were made members of the Corpus Christi Guild, walking in bright procession from the Holy Trinity Priory to the recently-completed Minster.

Consequently, when he was killed in battle against Henry Tudor at Bosworth in 1485, Yorkshire had once again backed the losing side: 'King Richard, late mercifully reigning upon us,' lamented the Aldermen of York, 'was piteously slain and murdered, to the great heaviness of this City.' The most serious of several risings against Henry VII, crowned soon after Bosworth, occurred in Yorkshire, but fizzled out for want of a leader. Henry offered a general pardon and, by marrying a daughter of Edward IV, united the red of Lancaster and the white of York in the Tudor rose. Less than two years later, when Lambert Simnel attempted a revolt against Henry, he received notably scant support from Yorkshire.

The Wars of the Roses left the North of England with a weakened, humbled nobility, and the authority of the sovereign replaced that of the great feudal lords. The advisory council established by Richard was moved from the Nevilles' old fortified home at Sheriff Hutton to urbane York where, as the Council of the North, it would administer the instructions of the London government till 1641. The country settled down to a period of comparative peace—excepting the paying off of sundry scores, like the murder of the Earl of Northumberland by a mob near Thirsk—discarding all former feuds in one last vigorous defeat of the traditional enemy, the Scots.

This was in 1513, when James IV of Scotland grasped an opportunity presented by the absence of the main English army in France, to cross into Northumberland, where he was met and in knightly fashion challenged to battle by a hastily-mustered English force at Flodden Field. A ballad, supposedly composed by a Yorkshire schoolmaster within a half-century of the event, paints a graphic picture of the peasantry preparing to follow their landlords to war:

> *Some made their battle-axes bright;*
> *Some from their bills did rub the rust;*
> *Some made long pikes and lances light,*
> *Some pikeforks for to join and thrust . . .*
> *The plowmen hard their teams could take*
> *And to hard harness them convert,*
> *Their shares defensive armour make,*
> *To save the head and shield the hert . . .*

Commander of a Yorkshire contingent was that same legendary

Henry Clifford 'conceal'd in shepherd's caul', long since restored to his estates:

> *From Penigent to Pendlehill,*
> *From Linton to Long Addingham,*
> *And all that Craven coasts did till,*
> *They with the lusty Clifford came . . .*

And at Flodden the Scots died in their thousands about the gashed body of their king.

Through such events, monastic life continued more or less unobtrusively, with a tendency for the smaller houses to become poor and the larger to grow rich, against a general relaxing of earlier ideals. Responsibility for teaching was slipping out of monastic into broader hands: in 1509 Hugo Goes had set up Yorkshire's first printing-press in the Minster Yard at York; 30 years later Yorkshire's Miles Coverdale published the first complete English translation of the Bible; to 46 Yorkshire grammar schools at the beginning of the sixteenth century were added another 68 by its close. The canons of once-wealthy Bolton were in debt; Arthington was valued at a miserable £11, Grosmont at £12, Esholt at £13, Ellerton-on-Swale at £15. On the other hand, the business successes of Cistercian abbeys like Fountains had brought, with prosperity, worldliness. If contemporary accounts of monastic corruption and immorality (one abbot was alleged to keep six mistresses) were highly coloured, there were many lesser indiscretions. Hunting formed a popular pastime; worship was neglected in favour of luxury and easy living. At Warter the canons sometimes slept off the premises, whilst the nuns at Nun Appleton went visiting an ale-house. The Egglestone monks were 'full of quarrelling among themselves'.

Antagonism towards a lax and worldly Church was nothing new. The North Yorkshire theologian and pamphleteer, John Wyclif, had passionately attacked his fourteenth-century contemporaries, sending out by way of counterpoise his own order of poor travelling priests, the Lollards. Wyclif had been condemned as a heretic for his pains, his very remains dug up and burnt and his ashes scattered: he would also be reverently called 'The Morning Star of the Reformation.'

Now, in 1529, Henry VIII began a series of measures by which he would replace the Pope as head of the Church in England. These included, notoriously, the Dissolution of the Monasteries, as centres of papal influence; though there seems little doubt that the appropriation of monastic revenues formed an important consideration. Houses were closed overbearingly and with unseemly haste. Within hours of entering Yorkshire at the beginning of 1536, Thomas Cromwell's agents were reporting 'gret corruption emongiste persons religious', and were expecting 'to fynde muche evile disposition both in the abbot and the convent' of St Mary's at York before they had even seen it. Within one short month, in the dead of winter, they had made a sketchy itinerary of the county which supposedly qualified them to allege 'manifest sin, vicious, carnal, and abominable living' in the smaller religious houses. The less scrupulous monastic inmates, too, could take politic advantage of the situation. A Ripon canon called Marmaduke Bradley bribed his way into Fountains, Cromwell's commissioners informing their master that he 'will give you six hundred marks to make him abbot there, and pay you immediately after the election, without delay or respite, at one payment. The first fruits to the King is a thousand pounds which he with his policy will pay within three years, and owe no man therefore one groat'. Having secured his position as Abbot of Fountains, Bradley was shortly able to surrender the house in return for a handsome pension.

Yet the Dissolution was not popular with the people of the North. Wrote the Yorkshire eye-witness of a typical scene: 'As soon as the visitors were entered within the gates, they called the abbot and other officers of the house, and caused them to deliver all the keys, and took an inventory of all their goods, both within doors and without. Such beasts, horses, sheep, and cattle as were abroad in pasture or grange places, the visitors caused to be brought into their presence. And when they had done so, they turned the abbot and all his convent and household forth out of the doors . . . It would have made a heart of flint melt and weep to have seen the breaking-up of the house, the sorrowful departing and the sudden spoil that fell the same day of their departure from their house.'

Northern opposition found an outlet in 1536, the year when the smaller monasteries were closed, in a rising known as the Pilgrimage of Grace which, in the few short weeks of its vitality,

20   *The Pilgrimage of Grace: a romanticised Victorian interpretation*

took York, Pontefract, Hull, Doncaster—in fact, virtually controlled the whole north-east from Lincolnshire to the Border; in Yorkshire, only Scarborough and Skipton Castles remained loyal and uncaptured. The Pilgrims' leader, lawyer Robert Aske, presented a list of demands to the King's negotiators: notably the reopening of the suppressed monasteries ('one of the beauties of this realm to all men and strangers passing through the same'), and the restoration of the Pope as head of the Church, together with a miscellany of social and political grievances indicative of the North's resentment of an increasingly centralized government. The King temporized, promised concessions which he had no intention of honouring, and the rising stagnated and dispersed. Whereupon, Henry ordered 'such dreadful execution to be done upon a good number of these habitants of every town and village that hath offended in this rebellion as well by the hanging of them upon trees as by the quartering of them and the setting up of their heads and quarters in every town great and small without pity or respect'. Two hundred and sixteen rebels and sympathisers, including the Prior of Bridlington and the Abbots of Fountains, Rievaulx and Jervaulx, were put to death; Aske was hanged in chains from the top of Clifford's Tower, one York market-day. When the King visited the north a few

21 *Rievaulx Abbey, as a picturesque nineteenth-century ruin.*

years later, he was met at Bawtry by 200 Yorkshire gentlemen and 4,000 'tall yeomen and serving-men well-horsed', who fell on their knees and tactfully presented him with £900. The citizens of York contributed a further £100; the mayor of Hull gave him a sword.

So the Dissolution continued: in 1539 it was the turn of the larger houses to close. The culture they had nurtured suffered an irrevocable spoliation. 'Every person,' an eye-witness succinctly noted, 'had everything good cheap.' Lead from the roofs was melted down on the spot; stained-glass windows were smashed for the sake of even their meagre lead. Woodwork was chopped up for lighting fires, or rotted exposed to the elements. Stone was carted away for rebuilding, like the use of Kirkstall stone for a Leeds bridge; bits of monasteries can be found embedded in barns and walls, where local farmers looted their remains—generally, houses in more remote areas, such as the great Cistercian abbeys, have survived more completely than those near towns. Pictures were destroyed, plate sold, stolen or lost. 'I do send to Your Majesty,' wrote the Duke of Norfolk, in the midst of energetic confiscations, 'all such things of gold as were on the Shrine at Bridlington which I caused Master Magnus to take of the said

Shrine at my being there to suppress the house; the said gold work is in two boxes sealed with my seal . . .' He went on to draw an extremely fine distinction: 'And if I durst be a thief, I would have stolen them to have sent them to the Queen's grace, but now your Highness having them may give them unto her without offence if it be your pleasure'! Priceless libraries were scattered to the winds, since outside the monasteries there was yet a limited public capable of appreciating them: illiterates acquired manuscripts, 'some to serve their cakes, some to scoure their candelstyckes, and some to rubbe their bootes'. When, under Edward vi, the English Reformation went a step further by abolishing the mass and removing shrines and altars, the waste and pillage spread to church treasures. 'What should I do?' one contemporary excused himself. 'Might I not, as well as others, have some profit of the spoil of the abbey? For I did see all would away, so I did as others did.'

At least, the Dissolution facilitated the emergence of a Tudor aristocracy from those loyal, opportunist or substantial families who were able to buy monastic lands cheaply. Fountains Abbey was sold to Sir Richard Gresham, Byland to Sir William Pickering; Cholmleys and Fairfaxes, Ramsdens and Ingrams acquired wide estates, and their solid residences, sometimes built from monastic stones, replaced the castles of the feudal barons as symbols of a new and peaceable influence and power. Almost at a stroke, Yorkshire had moved out of Medieval into modern times.

Not that the old savageries were by any means over, as Mary Tudor followed Edward vi and was followed in turn by Elizabeth i, and the official religion swayed from Protestant to Catholic and back again to a compromise Church of England. Incensed at government confiscation of chantry lands in 1549, a Seamer parish clerk and a yeoman led a rising, terrorised the locality for three months, murdered a commissioner and were duly hanged. Sir Thomas Stafford, heading a revolt against Mary in 1557, seized Scarborough Castle by disguising his men as peasants on market-day, and ruled as self-styled Protector of the Realm for precisely four days before capture and execution. Five hundred martyrs burnt at the stake under Mary included a former Prior of Nostell and an apprentice tallow-chandler from Kirkby Moorside; a Bedale man was burnt for heresy at Richmond. A situation which had at last grown dormant during the first decade of Queen

Elizabeth's reign, was excited afresh by the arrival in England of Mary, Queen of Scots, Catholic claimant to the throne and a natural focal point for plots against Elizabeth.

The Rising of the North erupted in 1569, ostensibly an attempt to restore Catholicism and secure Mary's succession, but in effect an indifferently-supported final throw, on the part of the Percies and Nevilles and other northern lords, to impose their will on London. The ill-starred venture caught the popular imagination and became celebrated in ballads:

> Att Whethersbye they mustered their men,
>   Upon a ffull fayre day;
> Thirteen thousand there were seene
>   To stand in battel ray.
>
> The Erle of Westmoreland, he had in his ancyent
>   The dunn bull in sight most hey,
> And three doggs with golden collers
>   Were sett out royallye.
>
> The Erle of Northumberland, he had in his ancyent
>   The halfe moone in sight soe hye,
> As the Lord was crucifyed on the crosse,
>   And set forthe pleasantlye.

The reality, however, was less glamorous than this gay flaunting of badges and banners, and the rebels mustered only an estimated

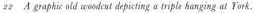

22   *A graphic old woodcut depicting a triple hanging at York.*

3,800 foot and 1,600 horse. To be sure, they celebrated Mass in Ripon Cathedral, and overturned the Communion table at Kirkby Moorside; but royalist garrisons held fast—with the exception of Barnard Castle, where 226 defenders jumped over the walls to join the rebels—blocking the roads south, and the Rising retreated and fell apart. Neville fled to Flanders, where the King of Spain provided him with a pension. Percy sought refuge with the Scots, who eventually sold him to the English for £2,000; he was duly executed at York and his head exposed in the traditional way over Micklegate Bar. The Nortons of Norton Conyers, the father and nine sons of whom had ridden out with the Rising, scattered or were killed, but found a posthumous glory in Wordsworth's poem, 'The White Doe of Rylstone'. Meanwhile, the poor suffered from the depredations of a royal army sent north to mop up. This was not the end of Catholic plots against the monarchy, and a Percy was to take part in the Guy Fawkes attempt to blow up James I's Parliament; but the military impotence of the northern lords had been effectively underlined.

If the official Elizabethan religion was a Church of England with the Queen as Supreme Head, the pious Catholic could still overtly hear mass; many, indeed, were prepared to suffer fines rather than attend the stipulated services. A list of those 'refusinge the churche and publique prayer' in the diocese of York, in 1577, contains upwards of 200 names, ranging from 'the olde Countesse of Cumbrelande' and 'olde Ladye Wharton', each worth £500 a year, to Elizabeth Ellerker, 'gentlewoman' with a bare £10 'in goods'; Henry Cumberforth, Bachelor of Divinity, 'worth nothinge, yet verie wilfull and a great perverter of others'; and John Brettan with his wife Francis, their worldly possessions 'nil'. It was at York in 1586 that Margaret Clitherow died for her faith and for harbouring priests, 'though no sufficient evidence could be produced to convince her guilty of the crime'. Indeed, recusancy seemed rather to grow more determined in the face of persecution. Meanwhile, the Anglican Church, through its parish units, became ever more integrally bound up with the life of the community, registering baptisms, marriages and burials, surveying highways, overseeing the poor, even appointing local constables.

For the Tudor age was witnessing gradual social and economic changes. York's wool trade slowly declined, stifled by guild regulations which limited the number of apprenticeships, created

23   *The Halifax Gibbet, with a malefactor on the point of decapitation.*

over-specialist classes—tailors, glovers, drapers and mercers all guarded jealously distinct roles—fixed measures and dimensions, and even restricted coverlet-weavers to a single loom and detailed the kinds of yarn they were allowed to use. Navigation of the Ouse was growing increasingly difficult, and Hull formed a more convenient merchant centre; whilst the Dissolution struck hard at the city's religious activities. Beverley similarly lapsed and, lacking the business provided at York by the presence of the Council of the North, fell into 'greate ruine and decaye, and specially in the pryncipalle and chief stretes there, . . . with pittys, sellers, and vaultes lying open and uncoveryd, very perilous for people who go by in the night'.

But York and Beverley's decline was the West Riding's gain, for there, in growing towns like Halifax, Leeds and Wakefield, 'the water-mylnes is nigh at hande', together with an increasing population of 'poore folke as speynners, carders, and other necessary work-folkes'. A basically cottage industry was fostered by the merchant clothiers who organised the flow of cloth from the weavers' often remote homes to markets and ports. The Halifax district grew rapidly to prominence, followed by Bradford, Leeds—notable for its 'art or mystery of making and working

woollen cloths, commonly called in English "Northern Dozens" '
—and Wakefield which, it was said under Henry VIII, 'standith
al by clothyng'. Halifax guarded its trade so zealously that anybody caught stealing cloth worth more than thirteen pence was
liable to summary execution by the gibbet, a 'keene edged
hatchet', in the graphic words of one contemporary, 'drawne up
by a pulley and a cord to ye crosse on ye topp, and the malefactor
layes his head on ye block below; then they let runne the stock
wth ye hatchet in, and dispatch him immediately'.

Sheffield's steel industry was well established: Chaucer had
described his miller of Trumpington as carrying a Sheffield
'whittle' or knife in his hose, and Elizabeth I's Lord Burghley was
presented with 'a case of Hallamshire whittles, being such
fruites as this pore cuntrey afordeth, with fame throughout the
realme'. To knives were eventually added shears and scythes,
sickles and razors; the Hallamshire Cutlers' Company was
founded in 1624, and 14 years later built its first stout Cutlers'
Hall of stone with a slate roof. Changing methods of smelting and
casting, together with a growing scarcity of wood for domestic
fuel as forests receded from populated areas, created an increasing
demand for a 'kind of stone, being impregnated with sulphur or
some fatty matter': South Yorkshire coal was proportionately
quarried and scratched up from shallow pits. Hull too was
developing, by means largely of a trade in dried fish from Iceland
and Yorkshire wool to Flanders, into a rich port 'with magnificent
buildings, strong fortifications, crowded ships, abundance of
merchants, and a great affluence of all things', its houses mainly
of brick and its streets paved with stones brought in as ballast.
Allied seafaring industries thrived, like cable-making and hemp-
winding. For awhile, Elizabethan Hull ranked as England's
second busiest outport, trading both with the Old and the New
Worlds, sending the first whalers to the Arctic and the first English-
men to Russia. To the north of the county, a 'great fisher town'
Whitby was emerging also as a coaling port; whilst at nearby
Guisborough, alum was mined.

The countryside was in process of transformation as Tudor
enclosures took a first toll of open fields and common lands. To
be sure, this would be on a modest scale compared with the great
eighteenth-century movement, and represented a logical attempt
to gear agriculture to the rising population; but the poor were

nevertheless resentful—Yorkshire saw no fewer than 16 agrarian riots between 1528 and 1547, and the Pilgrimage of Grace had put forward an unrealistic demand for the discontinuance of enclosures. Increased sheep farming was blamed for some unemployment. 'Your shepe,' Sir Thomas More wrote exaggeratedly, 'that were wont to be so meke and tame, and so smal eaters, now, as I heare saye, be become so great devowerers and so wylde, that they eate up, and swallow downe the very men them selfes. They consume, destroye, and devoure whole fields, howses, and cities.'

The authority of the manor-house had replaced that of the castle, each lord now urbanely judging his tenants' grievances and misdemeanours, issuing the edicts sufficient to his own little community, through his manor court. Surviving Elizabethan court rolls concern themselves largely with enclosures. At Haworth in the West Riding, one William Hopkinson was fined fourpence 'because he hath not maintained the dool fence at Westfelld heade'; John Sowden twelve pence 'because he hath driven cattle and sheep into the meadows of Haworth'; Henry Ackroyd had failed to 'sustain his fences', and Humphrey Toothill had 'broken the enclosure of his Lord'. There was friction with neighbouring Oxenhope, whose inhabitants were forbidden to 'place or drive their beasts or animals in the Lieshay graines'; likewise with Stanbury, tenants whereof repeatedly drove sheep 'from the Commons of Haworth'. For the rest, lords of the manor were expected to administer the minutiae of village life, preserving rights of way, restricting the indiscriminate cutting of wood, enforcing a proper ringing and yoking of swine.

Increased business and land speculations had given rise to a new peaceable gentry, its luckier members climbing upwards to aristocracy, whose homes reflect the changing pattern of the fifteenth and sixteenth centuries in bridging the transition from defensive quarters to comfortable, then luxurious, living: from the great square tower of Nappa Hall in Wensleydale, and the moated Markenfield Hall near Ripon, to the more spectacular designs of Burton Agnes and Burton Constable and the sheer magnificence of Temple Newsam House. The well-to-do cultivated a taste for refinements copied in part from the continent, and lavished their attention on ornamental chimney-pieces and plaster ceilings, wainscotted long galleries and small-paned glass windows. They patronised musicians and poets and painters, slept in four-poster beds and ate off a widening range of tableware; though they were reluctant to abandon that multi-purpose item of furniture, the large box or chest, and their sanitation remained primitive. And of course, little of this sophistication rubbed off on the lower classes. In Cleveland, when funeral parties were burying their dead, they sat up all night: 'some kneel down and pray by the corpse, some play at cards, some drink and take tobacco', indulging in 'mimical plays and sports' by blacking their hands, 'rubbing them under the bottom of the pot' and smutting the face of some 'simple young fellow' of their number; finally sending the deceased on his way with a dirge older than Protestant or Catholic or, indeed, than Christianity:

> *If ever thou gave either hosen or shoon,*
> *Every night and awle,*
> *Sitt thee downe and putt them on,*
> *And Christ receive thy Sawle.*

> *But if hosen nor shoon thou never gave nean,*
> *Every night and awle,*
> *The Whinnes shall prick thee to the bare beane,*
> *And Christ receive thy Sawle.*

Broadening horizons and the fabled opportunities of the Elizabethan era brought a variety of Yorkshiremen into national prominence. There was Roger Ascham of Kirby Wiske, near Thirsk, tutor to Elizabeth and 'a looker on in the Cokpit of learning thies many yeares', whose treatise on archery won him a pension from Henry VIII and whose book *The Scholemaster* became a classic teachers' manual. 'I would rather have thrown ten thousand pounds into the sea,' cried the Queen on his death, 'then have lost my Ascham . . .' There was Sir Martin Frobisher of Altofts, near Wakefield, who led three expeditions into the Arctic in courageous if futile search for the North-West Passage to a fabulous Cathay. His first, three tiny vessels and 35 men, was waved off by the Queen, sailing into an empty landscape 'encompassed with monstrous high islands of ice', where Frobisher captured and brought home an Eskimo who soon, however, died. Two later and bigger attempts wandered eerily among the icebergs, one ship colliding with a whale which 'thereat made a great and hideous noise, and casting up his body and tail, presently sank under water'. More successfully, Frobisher held a vital command in the defeat of the Armada; and received his death-wound fighting his Queen's Spanish foes. . . . And there was Christopher Saxton, cartographer, born between Leeds and Dewsbury, who first surveyed England and Wales from the vantage-points offered by 'any towre, castle, highe place or hill'. His atlas set the pattern in map-making for the next two centuries.

FURTHER READING

Chapter 4
Phyllis Bentley: *Colne Valley Cloth, from the Earliest Times to the Present Day*, 1947.
James J. Cartwright: *Chapters in the History of Yorkshire*, 1872.
A. H. Dodd: *Life in Elizabethan England*, 1961.
Charles A. Federer, editor: *The Ballad of Flodden Field: a Poem of the XVIth Century*, 1884.
J. S. Fletcher: *The Reformation in Northern England*, 1925.
J. C. Dickinson: *Monastic Life in Medieval England*, 1961.
Winifred I. Haward: *Yorkshire and the Wars of the Roses*, 1970.
Paul Murray Kendall: *Richard the Third*, 1955.
Alex. D. H. Leadman: *Battles Fought in Yorkshire*, 1891.
Michael Pocock: *The Tudors in Yorkshire*, 1970.
W. E. Tate: *The English Village Community and the Enclosure Movements*, 1967.
Clifford Whone, editor: *Court Rolls of the Manor of Haworth* (Bradford Historical and Antiquarian Society Local Record Series), 1946.

5
Stuart Yorkshire

By the time Charles I came to the throne in 1625, the surface stability achieved under Elizabeth was splintering. His father James I had quarrelled endlessly with a Parliament groping its way towards challenging the King's absolute authority. Extreme Protestants, the Puritans, were openly dissatisfied with the established Church, some of their ministers resigning rather than conform to the Prayer Book; on the other hand, many of the northern gentry were numbered amongst the Catholic recusants. There were confrontations over taxation, unsuccessful foreign policies, unpopular favourites . . . Charles's answer was to arrest political opponents, to dissolve antagonistic Parliaments, and from 1629 till 1640 he ruled without any Parliament at all. His agent Sir Thomas Wentworth, of Wentworth Woodhouse, near Rotherham, was made Lord President of the Council of the North which, from the rebuilt King's Manor at York, saw out its closing years as representative of a most absolute rule. Wentworth's measures at this period included a spirited attempt to keep the plague at bay, approaching York both from Lancashire and Lincolnshire, by 'inhibiting all the publicke faires hearabouts, wch might drawe a concourse of people togeither; our watches are very well and strickly kept in every place; all passadges betwixt us and Lincolnshire by water stopped as much as may be, to the intent that cumming by lande they may be a little better aired before they cum into any partt of this County; and the visited persons well provided not only for the necessities of nature, but of all such druggs and other medecins as the Phisitions advise to be good to preventt and correctt the malignity of this contagion'. Plague, indeed, was the recurring terror of this as of previous ages:

in 1604 it had killed 3,512 people in York and had forced the assizes to move temporarily to Wakefield.

Charles's personal rule stirred a hotbed of opposition. His marriage to French Catholic Henrietta Maria troubled the Protestants; increased fines for recusancy displeased the Catholics. Larger taxes on finished cloth alienated the clothing districts. His levying of ship money in peace-time and on inland towns was universally less than popular; though a table of amounts raised in 1635 offers an interesting comparison of relative assessments: York £520, Leeds £200, Hull £140, Doncaster £100, Pontefract £60, Richmond £50, Beverley £50, Ripon £40, Scarborough £30, Hedon £20. His attempts to impose the Anglican Prayer Book on the Presbyterian Scots inspired open rebellion, to counter which he was compelled in 1640 to summon the Short Parliament (immediately dissolved) and then the Long Parliament, which insisted on the impeachment and execution of Wentworth, now Earl of Strafford—'The authority of the King,' he had declared, 'is the keystone which closeth up the arch of order and government.' The abolition of the Council of the North soon followed.

The situation, whereby a determined Parliament composed for the most part of haughty gentry sought to limit the powers of a stubbornly autocratic monarch, could be resolved only by violence. As the country declined into civil war with, generally speaking, Catholics, Anglicans and aristocracy siding with the King, Puritans and gentry with Parliament, Yorkshiremen bandied increasingly virulent abuse: staunch Royalists called the Parliamentarians 'factious and seditious'; Parliamentarians retaliated with epithets like 'malignants' and 'desperate, bloody men'. Early in 1642 Charles abandoned a capital grown too hot for him and, appealing to the loyalty of his more northerly subjects, set up court at York. But Hull, strategically vital, strongly fortified and housing a substantial arsenal, refused to admit him; and though, when open hostilities were declared that summer, the majority of Yorkshire castles were garrisoned for the King, the coastal stronghold of Scarborough likewise remained in Parliamentary hands, ensuring Parliamentary control at sea.

The eventual defeat and execution of Charles 1 is a matter of well-worn history which need not concern us here. The Civil War's more outstanding Yorkshire features are confused episodes of street-fighting between bands of untrained men; the set-piece

24 *The King's Manor at York*

battle of Marston Moor; the besieging of castles never intended
for the age of gunpowder; and the emergence of several brilliant
personalities.

The early vicissitudes of Bradford are not untypical. There a
Parliamentary element were quick to seize the initiative and,
according to a young literate apprentice, 'we set about fortifying
ourselves with the greatest alacrity, resolution and assiduity,
in order, if possible, to frustrate every attempt that might be made
upon us to deprive us of our liberties and properties'. They had no
officers, no colours, no company formations, and could muster
no more than 80 men armed with muskets and fowling-pieces
(half of these borrowed from Halifax); the rest, possibly on the
underside of 200, equipped themselves with clubs, scythes, flails,
sickles mounted on poles. Late in 1642 they had thrown up street
barricades and prepared to resist the entry of a Royalist force
numbering, by various accounts, between 700 and 1,500, and
boasting two small artillery pieces and a partial uniform of buff

73

or red coats. The first clash was tentative: Royalist dragoons robbed a woman, killed two unarmed men, and withdrew when fired upon; their artillery lobbed, it is precisely chronicled, 17 shots against the parish church tower hung about for protection with woolpacks, before a lucky marksman stationed therein killed the master gunner. Despite short range and crowded streets nobody was otherwise hurt, and only a few houses hit—and that most seriously damaged belonged to a Royalist!

It was when the fighting moved in closer that it developed that especial savagery reserved for civil wars and amateur soldiers. Attempting to approach the church house by house, the Royalists met hand-to-hand opposition in the surrounding lanes and fields, where the traditional courtesies of war counted for little: a Royalist officer, sprinting down a hedge-side ahead of his men, ran into two Parliamentarians and 'cried out for quarter, and they poor men not knowing the meaning of it, said—"aye, they would quarter him," and so killed him' (next day the Royalists sent a trumpeter with a request for the body). Mauled, the Royalists retired towards Leeds, from which they were ejected the following month. But unwalled and vulnerable, the clothing towns were destined to change hands repeatedly. In 1643, 3,000 Parlia-

25   Civil War fighting at Bradford—the Parish Church protected by wool-packs

mentarians were defeated at Adwalton Moor and Bradford was again attacked by a vastly superior Royalist force, to suffer bombardment—'the elements being as it were on fire'—and occupation, valuables being stolen, furniture thrown into the streets, beds emptied of their feathers, livestock driven off. 'When the soldiers found any thing that was better than meal,' recorded Parliamentarian combatant Joseph Lister, 'they emptied the sacks, and put that which was better in them'; whereupon women would gather up the meal again, off the streets. During another particularly sharp engagement amongst some homely trenches and breastworks at Leeds, a 'pious minister from Halifax', among the first Parliamentarians to enter an abandoned Royalist position, 'immediately proceeded to praise God by singing the first verse of Psalm 68', adding further verses after each dash forward.

The battle of Marston Moor in July 1644, marked the Civil War's turning-point, followed as it was by the collapse of the Royalist centre at York. Yorkshire lore has made much of the attractive figure of Charles's nephew, the dashing cavalry commander Prince Rupert, chronicling the sites of the tented camps along his march; but at Marston Moor, between York and Wetherby, his troopers were outfought by the Ironsides drilled by a dour Huntingdonshire farmer-lawyer called Oliver Cromwell, whose 'God made them as stubble to our swords' would become the most-quoted statement of its time. Yet it was a close-run Parliamentary victory, with Cromwell wounded and a Wharfedale general, Sir Thomas Fairfax, tearing the identifying white favour from his hat and riding through the enemy lines to fetch reinforcements to a vital corner of the field. Dramatic episodes included a thunderstorm and the last magnificent stand of the crack Royalist Whitecoats. The surrender of York a fortnight later spelled the end of the Royalist cause in the North, as first the undefended towns, then the castles, passed under Parliamentary control.

Parliament's often lengthy sieges of Medieval castles were occasioned by a curiously fastidious observance of gentlemanly rules of war, by which the defenders of honourably surrendered strongpoints were allowed to continue the struggle from a new position: the York garrison, for example, retained their arms and were given safe conduct to Skipton 'or the next Garrison Towne within sixteene miles of the Princes Army'. The latest siege

26 *Major-General John Lambert (1619–1683)*

techniques, when tardily brought to bear, either forced a quick capitulation or proved strangely ineffective. Hence, Helmsley Castle held out for some months despite residential additions jeopardising its defence; Pontefract withstood artillery and mining and the breaching of its Piper Tower; Scarborough (which had transferred its allegiance from Parliament to King) survived a year's harassment from both land and sea, including a three-day bombardment which split its keep in two, its thereby unroofed officers having 'to betake themselves to poore cabins reared against the walls and banckes in the Castle yeard'; Skipton held out for three years.

The epic of Skipton, the Cliffords' old castle astride the Aire Gap, is not so much one of siege as of intermittent blockade despite which its defenders were able to collect rents up the Dales, send out an abortive relief force to Helmsley, and launch cavalry raids on Parliamentary forces at Thornton and Keighley. The

Parish Register (unashamedly partisan, referring to the Parliamentarians as 'rebels') tersely chronicles the mingling of town and garrison and the wartime fathering of children: 'Donkin Leedale Gunner at skipton Castle' had a son who died within six months; whilst 'Ann a basterd' of soldier Thomas Kidd and 'one Nell Garnet' was both baptised and buried in just eight days. But largely the Register records violent death: 'Tho. Hall a trooper unfortunatly slayne by a pistole', John Hargraves found dead atop Rombalds Moor, soldiers from 'darbishyre' and 'leverpoole' and Northumberland, sometimes nameless, carried wounded from Marston Moor to die in Skipton's walls; and Major John Hughes, deputy commander, fatally injured in a sally and 'a most valiant souldier'. Closer and more determined siege operations in midsummer of 1645 signalled an inevitable end, however, and Skipton surrendered just before Christmas, the last Royalist castle in Yorkshire.

The Civil War swept into military prominence, especially on the Parliamentary side, a number of country gentlemen who would otherwise have remained in unexceptional obscurity. John Lambert, of Calton, near Kirkby Malham, was involved both in the siege of Skipton and the seesawing struggles for Bradford, and had a horse killed under him at Marston Moor, distinguishing himself chiefly in the latter stages of the war against the Royalist Scots. 'Such was the gallantry of Major-General Lambert,' it was written of one engagement in 1651, 'that had it not been for his armour he had been lost, a brace of bullets being found between his coat and his arms.' He climaxed his military with a political career.

But Yorkshire's arguably outstanding figure was Sir Thomas Fairfax, scholar and soldier of Denton in Wharfedale, who had seen continental campaigning in the Thirty Years' War and whose humble desire was to be 'someway serviceable to the Public'. If he commanded at Parliament's only notable Yorkshire defeat at Adwalton Moor, his name also features in almost every major and ultimately successful Parliamentary stratagem of the northern Civil War: he fought at Leeds and Wakefield and Selby, was besieged in Hull and in turn helped lay siege to York and Helmsley and Pontefract; at Marston Moor he rallied the wavering Parliamentary army. In 1645, repeatedly wounded, his persistent devotion to his cause won him command of the New Model

27 Yorkshire's outstanding Parliamentary general, Sir Thomas Fairfax (1612–1671). From the painting by Robert Walker

Army which finished the war. Even his enemies respected him: Prince Rupert, marching to Marston Moor, billeted himself in Fairfax's home and courteously forbade pillaging—no mean gesture, in an age when loot was regarded as a legitimate perquisite for under-trained soldiery. Fairfax reciprocated by protecting York Minster's stained glass and, though he was not quick enough to prevent the blowing up of a monastic library in St Mary's Tower, offered rewards for manuscripts salvaged from the rubble. Characteristically, once the war was won, Fairfax refused any truck with the trial and execution of his King, retiring amongst his books and collections to his house at Nun Appleton, whence he strikingly emerged only to propose the restoration of Charles II following the collapse of the Commonwealth in 1660.

The close of the Civil War found a Yorkshire depressed and battle-worn. Its castles, those old symbols of baronial power, were finally rendered military untenable, slighted and dismantled. Pontefract was demolished and its very debris buried; Knaresborough was sold stone by stone, Skipton's towers reduced in height. A distraught resident of Wressle told its absent steward how workmen were 'with much violence' defacing the 'stately structure': 'Believe it, Sir, his Lordship hath sustain'd very deep losses in this house; I conceive 2000£ will not repair the ruins here.' Doughty Lady Anne Clifford alone faced up to Cromwell's ire, seeing her Skipton Castle and four others in Westmorland damaged and threatened with demolition. 'Let him destroy them if he will,' she proclaimed, 'but he shall surely find that as often as he destroys them I will rebuild them, while he leaves me a shilling in my pocket.' And Cromwell (not unaccustomed to bold Yorkshire women, having reputedly been confronted with a brace of pistols in the hands of Lady Ingilby of Ripley) replied: 'Let her build what she will, she shall have no hindrance from me.'

There were more serious after-effects. Yorkshire's wool trade had suffered. The West Riding clothing towns were battered, and to the ravages of war were added those of pestilence. Populations were decimated; grass grew in the streets of Leeds, and its markets moved out to Hunslet Moor and Chapeltown Green, where traders had to soak their cloth for two days before dealing. Commerce through York and Hull was sadly interrupted, and Holderness had been twice flooded during siege operations. Exports declined; piracy was rife in the North Sea. The roads southwards were dangerous and uncertain; though at least one cloth-merchant, Thomas Priestley of Soyland, near Halifax, maintained a regular packhorse traffic with London and gained thereby a name for resolution plus a worthwhile £20 profit on each trip. Only Sheffield had prospered by the war, its ironworks having contrived to supply cannonballs to both sides. Recovery came but slowly, the Commonwealth government making no considerable improvement, so that 'the particular Decay and Ruine of the Clothing Trade of this County' became one of Yorkshire's chief reasons for welcoming the Restoration. In 1666 Charles II's Parliament sought to create a demand by ordaining that every corpse should be buried in a woollen shroud, on pain of a fine; which occasioned a series of quaint albeit grisly entries in parish registers: 'Mary Higgins, of Allerton, makes oath that May Mitchell, of the same place, was not wrapt in any sheet or shroud but that was made of sheep's wool only as by Act of Parliament decreed.'

With Parliament's victory, the Puritans gained a temporary ascendancy and forbade Anglican worship, to fall themselves, at the Restoration, just as surely into disfavour; for the Common-wealth and Cromwell's Protectorate attempted an ill-advised meddling with people's habits and pleasures. Laws were framed against drunkenness and breaking the Sabbath, against gambling and swearing, sports and merry-making—and the Stuart age, by and large, could be very merry indeed. An itinerant rhymster rejoicing in the soubriquet Drunken Barnaby

(Barnaby, Barnaby, thou'st been drinking,
I can tell by thy nose and thy eyes winking.
Drunk at Richmond, drunk at Dover,
Drunk at Newcastle, and drunk all over)

had wenched and boozed his way about the realm prior to the Civil War, and had fared as merrily in Yorkshire as anywhere, and noted sundry 'jovial, jocund, jolly bowlers, as they were the world's controllers'. Bull-baiting always attracted an excited crowd, the barbarity of this old English sport nowise excused by a 'vulgar notion' that 'the flesh was not fit for use, unless the animal had been baited, or worried with dogs'.

28   Rev. Oliver Heywood, Northowram Nonconformist and diarist (1630–1702)

No more graphic picture of the profligacies of the times survives
than in the disapproving diaries of the Rev. Oliver Heywood, a
Northowram Nonconformist minister ejected from his chapel in
1662 and thereafter indomitably travelling about the county
preaching in private houses. At Haworth Tide he witnessed
'multitudes of people meet, feast, drink, play, and commit many
outrages in revellings, in rantings, riding, without any fear or
restraint'. At Halifax they were cock-fighting, 'and the Halifax
cocks generally beat the gentlemens, then on the wednesday,

29 *A pastoral Stuart scene.*

thursday, friday the gentlemens cocks fought, abundance of money was lost and won,—they drunk all night and were so high in swearing, ranting at the Crosse that they were heard far in the town'. Four men in Bradford 'killed themselves with drinking' in three months; whilst an ale-house 'in the great high road' between Bradford and Halifax boasted 'an abominable filthy sign' depicting a naked man and woman 'in a shameful manner' ('oh prodigious!'). At Denholme—'a very ignorant and prophane place'— an old man supposedly ripe for conversion fell unhappily foul of some fiddlers and idle company on his way to a prayer-meeting ('oh dreadful state!').

Entertainment extended to a range of cruel rowdy punishments. There was the pillory, prominent in many markets: in 1677 one James Ollerton, 'a common mover of suits and quarrels in disturbance of the peace', was made to stand successively in the pillories of Leeds, Bradford and Halifax; a forger was similarly exhibited at Bedale, Richmond and Middleham with his forgery stuck in the front of his hat. Rogues and vagabonds were publicly whipped, sometimes tied to posts and sometimes at a cart-tail: in 1622 '6 wanderers' were whipped all the way from Barnsley to Ardsley. Drunkards could be set in the stocks (an Act of 1605 stipulated a six-hour stint or a five-shilling fine which persisted until the mid-nineteenth century); whilst Wakefield Cathedral boasted a Scottish variant, the jougs, for chaining unruly worshippers by the neck. Scolds and gossips had their heads enclosed and their tongues clamped in a cage called a brank or bridle, and often women were subjected to the ducking-stool wheeled to a convenient depth of water. At Leeds, in 1694, Anne Saul, 'a person of lewd behaviour', was ducked 'for daily making strife and discord amongst her neighbours'. In Beverley they also ducked brewers of bad beer and bakers of bad bread; though such offenders usually suffered exposure in the cucking-stool, a chair without a seat in which they were carried through the streets, 'and the rest must not be stated,' apologises a Victorian writer on Wakefield, 'so depraved were the exhibitions of those times'. Crime proper was solidly punished by the gallows. One sensational murder case became immortalised in a play, *A Yorkshire Tragedy*, thinly attributed to Shakespeare. In 1604, Walter Calverley, of Calverley, near Bradford, irked by debts, dissipation and hints

30 Punishment for scolds and gossips — the brank

that his children 'were not by him begotten', had gone out of his mind, stabbed two of his sons to death and attempted to kill his wife. He suffered the fate reserved for unfortunates refusing to plead either guilty or not guilty, by being pressed to death at York Castle. This, the 'peine forte et dure', could take several days, and Calverley's request to be crushed more quickly was enshrined in a local saying: 'A pund of more weight, lig on, lig on!'

Witches, in an age which recognised a potent Devil, could be hysterically dealt with. Wrote an opponent of the Puritan Witch-Finder General, Matthew Hopkins: 'Every old woman with a wrinkled face, a furred brow, a hairy lip, a gobber tooth, a squint eye, a squeaking voice, or a scolding tongue, having a rugged coat on her back, a skull-cap on her head, a spindle in her hand, and a dog or cat by her side, is not only suspected, but pronounced a witch.' Women, and sometimes men, were dropped into rivers to see whether or not they would float, kept awake for days and made to repeat the Lord's Prayer, when a single hesitation meant guilt, stuck with pins in search of the 'witch's mark' whereby they were thought to suckle their familiars or imps—any wart would suffice. To be sure, the North's most notorious Stuart cases occurred just over the Lancashire border, in Pendle Forest, but Yorkshire was by no means immune. Six witches were executed at York in 1622. A wretched 'Old Wife Green' was lynched at Pocklington in 1631 and burnt alive by a furious mob. A woman believed to have thrown a man into fits at Wakefield was dragged from her home and beaten to death, and a Woodhouse couple were hanged for digging up corpses and invoking evil spirits. At York in 1648 Isabella Billington was more justifiably hanged and her body burnt, for crucifying her mother and sacrificing a calf and a cock to Satan. Knaresborough's Mother Shipton, a woman 'larger than common, her body crooked, her face frightful', seems to have devoted her 'extraordinary understanding' to predictions of varying accuracy:

Carriages without horses shall go,
And accidents fill the world with woe.
Around the world thoughts shall fly
In the twinkling of an eye . . .
The world to an end shall come,
In eighteen hundred and eighty-one.

84

31   A famous Yorkshire witch, Mother Shipton, from an engraving of 1663

But out of this period of strife and religious bigotry, of coarseness and superstition, shone redeeming features. In 1643 George Fox of Leicestershire had commenced his zealous travels about the country, preaching his Quaker message of God's spirit within man himself rather than in the outward show of established churches or 'steeple-houses'. By the following decade he was frequently in Yorkshire. When he tried to open a discussion in York Minster, the congregation threw him down the steps; butchers at Halifax broke up a meeting and swore they would kill him; at Doncaster he was dragged before the magistrates and stoned down the street. In Beverley, at least, 'the power of the Lord' felt so strong in him that nobody meddled with him, and one woman thought he was 'an angel'. Fox's readiest converts came, however, from the countryside and especially from the more remote Yorkshire dales, appropriately from landscapes of quiet farmsteads and high places: it was 'about Wensleydale and Sedbergh', in 1652, that he experienced a vision of 'a great people in white raiment by a river side, coming to the Lord'. Prior to the Toleration Act of 1689, the Quakers were persecuted for their faith, suffering imprisonment and the confiscation of their goods; despite which, the Society of Friends' first Yearly Meeting was held near Skipton in 1658, to consider overseas missionary work; whilst one of their earliest meeting-houses, at Brigflatts, near Sedbergh, attracted an estimated 600 worshippers in 1677.

Education was coming, however shakily, within the scope of some at least of the poorer classes, as increasingly the benefactions of the comparatively well-to-do included the endowment of free schools. £10 from Henry Fawcett in 1619 financed the minister of Halton Gill 'for teaching poor men's children in Arncliffe'. At Bridlington in 1636, William Hustler 'gave a rentcharge of £40' towards educating 20 poor children; whilst Arkingarthdale Grammar School grew out of John Bathurst's modest £16 for a schoolmaster in 1659 (he left another £4 for apprenticing a poor boy of the parish). Thomas Keresforth willed £19 15*s* 2½*d* a year for school use at Barnsley in 1660; and the rents from William Hutchinson's farm at Sleightholme in 1693 paid a master and an usher at Bowes, provided a schoolhouse and even the coals to heat it with. In 1669 Charles Read bequeathed a spectacular £2,000 'to be laid out in land of the annual value of £120, for the support of the school and almshouses erected by him in Drax'.

Literature reached a fruition. If London's Parliamentary Civil War found employment for John Milton, Yorkshire's nurtured the Hull metaphysical poet, Andrew Marvell. His political satires, his diplomatic travels in Holland, Sweden and Russia, his serious role as Member of Parliament for Hull—all are forgotten: Marvell's immortality rests on the poems he wrote in Fairfax's garden at Nun Appleton, where he was tutor to the general's daughter Mary and where his lyrical appreciation of Nature foreshadowed Clare and Wordsworth by a century and a half:

> *And, if at Noon my toil me heat,*
> *The Sun himself licks off my sweat.*
> *While, going home, the Ev'ning sweet*
> *In cowslip-water bathes my feet.*

Another, more homely literature raised itself out of an oral tradition of anonymous rhymes and jingles in 1683, when George Meriton, a Northallerton lawyer and author of such forbidding treatises as 'A Compendium of the Penal Laws now in

Force against Idleness, Profaneness, and Drunkenness', published his *Yorkshire Dialogue*—

> *Mother our Croky's Cawven sine't grew dark,*
> *And Ise flaid to come nar, she macks sike wark*—

and helped inaugurate a prolific vein of earthy dialect writing.

From Yorkshire too went William Congreve, born at Bardsey, to study briefly at the Middle Temple, plunge instead into London society, and become the Restoration's foremost dramatist. Truer, however, to his origins was Ralph Thoresby (born at Leeds, 1658; died at Leeds, 1725), antiquary, topographer and diarist who spans the transition from Stuart to Georgian periods. 'Preparing for a journey to York,' he recorded (in Leeds) in 1708: 'Lord, grant this favourable presence from sin and all dangers. We found the way very deep, and in some places dangerous for a coach that we walked on foot, but the Lord preserved us from all evil accident, that we got to our journey's end in safety, blessed be God.'

Roads, indeed, were haphazard in the extreme, maintained, or conversely neglected, by the parishes through which they passed. 'Narrow and rugged,' according to one traveller, 'with deep

32 View of Ralph Thoresby's Leeds from his Ducatus Leodiensis

87

ruts', they threaded a landscape still largely unenclosed and imprecisely mapped, albeit stripped by now of its potentially more savage ecological elements—John of Gaunt is credited with having killed the last wolf in the Leeds area—though as late as 1691 the churchwardens at Ilkley were paying an eightpenny bounty on wild-cat heads. Horseback and feet remained the surest means of transport, and goods went chiefly by packhorses, more generally known as bell-horses through the lead animal wearing a bell to warn anybody ahead to get out of the way, since bell-horses notoriously kept to the path and 'forced therefrom travellers of every description'. Drovers, too, were a common sight in Yorkshire, walking cattle shod against the changeable ground down from Scotland to the markets of London and the south. Often they followed ancient tracks and Roman roads, their parallel lines of livestock wearing broad ways in a direction roughly north to south. One drovers' route entered Yorkshire at Yarm-on-Tees and led by way of the Hambleton and Howardian Hills to York; another went through Catterick and Boroughbridge to Doncaster; others zig-zagged along lonely dales with vigorous old names like Mallerstang and Arkengarth, by Beckermonds and Yockenthwaite, accounting for weather-beaten inns in scarcely accessible places.

Yet intrepid and literate travellers of the period portray a growing urbanity in the towns and villages between their 'hideous' roads and 'rotten' moors. Thoresby, who journeyed extensively though preferring horseback to the 'effeminacy' of coaches, noted the numerous free schools and 'hospitals' provided by local benefactors. The latter were more properly almshouses: one at Waddington kept 'ten widows, and a chaplain to read prayers to them forenoon and after'; three 'poor widows' received 'each 40s, per annum' and their board in another at Bedale; and at Firby was 'an hospital built by Mr Chapman for six poor old men, and a master, who have each 5s per month (two pence per day), beside coats, caps, gowns, etc.'. The health-restoring waters at Yorkshire spas were becoming popular. Drunken Barnaby had 'paid two farthings to the keeper' of Robin Hood's Well at Skelbrook half-a-century before; by the 1690s a peripatetic hypochondriac called Celia Fiennes was engagingly recording her visits to a whole series. At the Harrogate 'Sulphur or Stincking spaw' she drank two quarts and found them 'a good sort of purge,

33 Packhorses and travellers following a Roman road across Bramham Moor.

if you can hold your breath so as to drink them down' (her horse, however, stoutly refused to follow her example). A 'spaw well' on the beach at Scarborough was covered by the sea at high tide, leaving 'a brackish and saltness which makes it purge pretty much'; and a spring at Copgrove 'must needs be very strengthening, it shutts up the pores of the body immeadiately so fortifyes from cold'. It was Celia Fiennes, an appreciative eater and drinker ('their ale is very strong') for all her spa preoccupations, who observed a heartening market-day custom at 'the sign of the Bush' in Leeds, whereby 'anybody that will goe and call for one tankard of ale and a pint of wine and pay for these only, shall be set to a table with 2 or 3 dishes of good meate and a dish of sweet-meates after'.

Following the Restoration, Yorkshire played little part in political events, beyond an abortive Farnley Wood Plot of 1663 which resulted in nothing but the execution of 21 of its handful of disappointed Parliamentarian conspirators. Indeed, as London increasingly acquired the sophistication and the magnetism befitting its capital status, the North, provincial, raided and fought over through recent centuries, slipped naturally into a less flamboyant role. The typical Yorkshire building of the age was not the palatial residence of its nobility; rather, the sturdy stone dwelling of its honest tradesmen, their initials proudly carved

34 *Date and initials—C.I.B. 1656—carved above a door at Embsay*

35 *Bolling Hall, Bradford*

above the door and a dab of ornamental plasterwork about the fireplace; and the fine but noway grandiose home—Shibden Hall, Halifax; Bolling Hall, Bradford; East Riddlesden Hall, Keighley—of its lesser gentry, its yeomen and, significantly, its merchants and clothiers who had made good.

FURTHER READING

Chapter 5
William Andrews: *Bygone Punishments*, 1931.
A. C. Cawley, editor: *George Meriton's 'A Yorkshire Dialogue' (1683)*, 1959.
Patricia Crowther: *Witchcraft in Yorkshire*, 1973.
George Fox: *The Journal of George Fox; being an Historical Account of his Life, Travels, Sufferings, and Christian Experiences*, 1901.
Winifred I. Haward: *Yorkshire and the Civil War*, 1971.
J. Horsfall Turner, editor: *The Rev. Oliver Heywood, B.A., 1630–1702: His Autobiography, Diaries, Anecdote and Event Books*, 1881–83.
Joseph Lister: *The Autobiography of Joseph Lister, of Bradford in Yorkshire*, edited by Thomas Wright, 1842.

6
The Eighteenth Century

In 1724 the prolific Daniel Defoe commenced—insofar as he is to be believed, perhaps, for he was a most plausible literary liar!— his exhaustive *Tour through the Whole Island of Great Britain*, and immortalised, among other things, his vigorous impressions of early Georgian Yorkshire. Happily, Defoe was not overly addicted to the preoccupations of so many eighteenth-century topographers. He did not dote on stately homes, though he saw the Earl of Carlisle's Castle Howard under construction to 'by far the finest design'. Nor did he pretend to a knowledge of antiquities: when shown 'some old Roman coins' at Tadcaster, he merely thought them 'so very much defaced with age, that we could read but D O, and A V, at a distance'. He was not even moved by the current vogue for 'spaws', and when his Knaresborough landlord proudly pointed out four different springs rising close together and asked, 'But is it not a strange thing, sir?' he coolly replied, being 'surfeited with country wonders', that in Derbyshire he had seen a hot and a cold spring side by side. Defoe's concern was rather to present a discursive 'view of the whole in its present state'—the county being so extensive that he had to make three journeys through it— 'as also of the commerce'.

The North Riding he thinks notable for 'the best and largest oxen, and the finest galloping horses'; the Bedale district is full of grooms, jockeys and breeders, whilst Northallerton Fair eight times a year attracts 'incredible' numbers of 'noble' oxen customarily sold into Lincolnshire. Richmond is a thriving market town and centre for the Wensleydale and Swaledale stocking trade— 'the smallest siz'd stockings for children are here sold for eighteen pence per dozen, or three half pence a pair, sometimes less'.

In the East Riding 'they feed great numbers of sheep, and breed also a great many black cattle and horses', though the interior landscape is 'very thin of towns' and along 30 miles of the coast he finds 'nothing remarkable'. Essentially a 'townee', Defoe prefers the bustle of population, and his keen journalistic eye selects the relevant details: 'very good ships for the coal trade' being built at Whitby; colliers putting into Bridlington in bad weather; Scarborough's popularity as a spa town, with 'a great deal of good company here drinking the waters' alongside a plentiful fishing industry; and Hull busily exporting 'all the trade at Leeds, Wakefield and Hallifax'.

On the West Riding, indeed, Defoe lavishes most of his prose, picturing the activity, already extensive, of a region still innocent, by half a century, of the Industrial Revolution, having 'the greatest towns in it, and the greatest number of them; the greatest manufactures, and consequently the greatest share of wealth, as it has also of people'. His ride into the Calder Valley over Blackstone Edge in an August blizzard understandably unnerved him, as did a terrain wherein 'no sooner we were down one hill but we mounted another'; yet he was able to observe dwellings and their

36 Cottage industry: women spinning

93

37 *Hull docks*

small acres of land dotted along the hillsides, and villages thick
in the valley-bottoms, whilst 'almost at every house there was a
tenter, and almost on every tenter a piece of cloth'; a profusion of
streams meanwhile running through dying-mills and scouring-
shops which 'emitted the water again, ting'd with the drugs of the
dying fat, and with the oil, the soap, the tallow, and other
ingredients used by the clothiers in dressing and scouring'.
Through the doors of 'master manufacturers' he glimpsed 'lusty
fellows, some at the dye-fat, some dressing the cloths, some in the
loom, some one thing, some another, all hard at work'.

Halifax struck him as being the energetic focus of a commerce
'not to be equalled in England'—which argues either a rapid
growth, or the extreme subjectivity of personal impressions,
since only three decades earlier Celia Fiennes had thought
Halifax 'almost ruined, and come to decay'; and to roughly this
period belongs a jingle on the comparative merits of the town and
a neighbour:

> *Halifax is built of wax,*
> *Heptonstall o' stooan:*
> *I' Halifax ther's bonny lasses,*
> *I' Heptonstall ther's nooan.*

Defoe ascribes this recent prosperity to the supplying of kersies—

a coarse woollen cloth—to armies abroad. Travelling on towards Leeds, he recorded a busy and 'infinitely populous' locality, Leeds itself presenting 'a noble scene of industry and application'. Its cloth market was held twice a week, with rows of trestles set up in the street and the clothiers bringing in their pieces for seven o'clock in the morning, when the ringing of the market bell signalled the spreading of pieces along the trestles, 'and behind every piece of cloth, the clothier standing to sell it. As soon as the bell has done ringing, the merchants and factors, and buyers of all sorts, come down, and coming along the spaces between the rows of boards, they walk up the rows, and down as their occasions direct. Some of them have their foreign letters of orders, with patterns seal'd on them, in rows, in their hands; and with those they match colours, holding them to the cloths as they think they agree to; when they see any cloths to their colours, or that suit their occasions, they reach over to the clothier and whisper, and in the fewest words imaginable the price is stated; one asks, the other bids; and 'tis agree, or not agree, in a moment.'

A similar degree of activity characterized South Yorkshire. Doncaster was 'a noble, large, spacious town, exceeding populous, and a great manufacturing town, principally for knitting'; Sheffield houses were blackened by the smoke of forges working day and night, turning out axes, knives and edged tools; Black Barnsley was also 'eminent' for iron and steel. The street trading witnessed by Defoe would move indoors a generation later— Leeds Coloured Cloth Hall was built in 1758, its White Cloth Hall in 1775; Bradford's Piece Hall opened in 1773, Halifax's in 1780.

Even by the early eighteenth century, therefore, the pace of industry was accelerating towards its Revolution. But other important developments preceded this. An increasing traffic in wheeled vehicles demanded an improvement of roads typically described as 'in a very ruinous Condition, and, in some Places, not only very narrow and incommodious, but almost impassable for Wheel-carriages, and sometimes very dangerous for Travellers'. Private enterprise took action in the shape of turnpike trustees, bodies of local landowners and gentry who obtained Acts of Parliament enabling them to repair existing roads, erecting tollbars and levying tolls for their maintenance. By Defoe's time, a number of trusts had been formed, for 'those dirty deep

38   *The Coloured Cloth Hall, Leeds*

roads' from London to the Midlands; but it was 1735 before
Yorkshire's first Turnpike Act, relating to the roads from Manchester and Oldham to Saddleworth, and from Rochdale over
Blackstone Edge to Halifax and Elland. Six more Acts in 1741
linked Doncaster, Wakefield, Leeds and Halifax with Lancashire
in the west and the Great North Road to the east; many others
followed. The journey from York to London, eight days in the
1670s, was reduced to less than two by the 1770s; Leeds to
London, two and a half days in 1768, took 20 hours by 1815.

Yet improvements fostered by the turnpike system could be
cautious, slow, uneven and not universally popular, for the confused poor of this expanding era tended to view any change as a
threat to their precarious existence. In 1753 a Leeds mob attacked
a new tollbar at Harewood and were beaten off by Edwin Lascelles, Esquire, with a force of his tenants. Shortly afterwards, a
truculent carter refusing to pay toll at Beeston was arrested but
immediately rescued by sympathisers, who proceeded to march
on the King's Arms Inn at Leeds Briggate, where three similar
non-payers were being held under military guard. There, a
rabble tore up the pavement, broke windows and shutters,
stoned the soldiers and knocked down a sentry; whereupon the
troops opened fire, killing eight and wounding 24 rioters.

Yorkshire's most remarkable contractor for the building of turnpike roads was John Metcalf, blinded by smallpox at the age of six and thereby known as Blind Jack of Knaresborough. His handicap notwithstanding, he learned to ride, swim, fish and play the fiddle, guided benighted travellers about the abysmal tracks of the Forest of Knaresborough, got involved with two women at once, eloped with one of them, served in the '45 Rebellion, dealt in fish, and in 1754 began his more personal association with roads when he inaugurated a stage-waggon between York and Knaresborough, which believably 'impressed upon him the appalling condition' of the King's highway. The early turnpike trustees expected no particular scientific method of their contractors, and Blind Jack, willing to turn his hand to anything, was able to build some 180 miles of road in Yorkshire and adjoining counties, including sections of those from Harrogate to Boroughbridge, Huddersfield to Halifax, Knaresborough to Wetherby, Wakefield to Dewsbury, Wakefield to Huddersfield . . . the latter entailing a difficult stretch across boggy ground, which he accomplished by instructing 60 men 'to pull and bind heather, or ling, in round bundles, and to lay it on the intended road in rows, and laying another across, pressing them well down; he then brought broad wheeled carriages'—that is, carts—'to lead stone and gravel for covering'. Passing clothiers on their way to Huddersfield market scoffed at him (his employers' intention had been 'to dig the earth quite out of the marshes, until they came to a solid bottom'), and when 'the first load was laid on, and the horses had gone off in safety, the company huzzaed from surprise'. This piece of road, it was recorded, 'needed no repairs for twelve years afterwards'. Blind Jack died in 1810, aged 92.

Alongside road developments came the canals, arguably an even more important means of transport in the North's economic growth and the very 'arteries of the Industrial Revolution'. Of course, the use of inland waterways was by no means new, least of all in Yorkshire with its rivers—Aire and Wharfe and Calder, Don and Ouse, Derwent and Hull—flowing ultimately into the Humber. 'Englond hath three Ryverse with in hym selffe comynge owte of the See in to the myddes of the londe,' Sir John Fortescue had written in 1451. 'The fyrst Ryver ys callyd Humber, that comyth uppe to Yorke and so forth uppe into the contrey.' Roman and Medieval York, indeed, had owed much of its influence

39   John Metcalf, 'Blind Jack of Knaresborough', roadmaker extraordinary, from an 1804 biography

to the navigability of the Ouse: its fourteenth-century exports and imports had included alum, wool, cloth, lead, stone, sea-coal, madder, linen, grain, wax, iron, timber, salt and spices. Beverley merchants, too, had deepened a creek providing a connection with the Hull; the Derwent and the Don, and a portion at least of the Aire, also carried Medieval traffic. But the increasing draught of sea-going vessels, combined with the hazards natural to estuaries, had hastened the decline of York and Beverley in favour of Kingston-upon-Hull; rivers had silted up. In 1699, however, a reawakening interest led to the formation of the Aire and Calder Navigation Company, by which these rivers—through a series of locks, cuts and scourings—were made respectively navigable as far as Leeds and Wakefield. Acts of 1701 and 1720 improved the Derwent and the Idle, and by 1725 Defoe was able to paint glowing pictures of the river trade, not only of Leeds, Wakefield and Bawtry, but also of York, where 'ships of any burthen come up within 30 mile of the city, and small craft from 60 to 80 ton, and under, come up to the very city'.

But it was a further development, the linking of navigable rivers and their Lancashire counterparts by canals, which opened up areas hitherto difficult of access and ensured steady transport between industries and ports. Whereas a packhorse had carried an approximate eighth of a ton, a single barge-horse—or, where tow-paths were deficient and human labour was cheap, a gang of 'halers' or men with a rope—could pull 30 tons. So the eighteenth

40   The Aire and Calder Navigation at Leeds

41   The five-rise locks on the Leeds and Liverpool Canal at Bingley

century witnessed a new form of labourer, the 'navigator' employed in digging or improving 'navigations' and henceforth known as the 'navvy', armies of whom, sweating, drinking and fighting, cut their deep fresh gashes across the countryside.

The efforts of almost a century, up to about 1830, resulted in a complex of waterways. The Aire and the Ouse were connected at Selby, later at Goole. The Barnsley Canal from Wakefield, and the Dearn and Dove Canal from Swinton, met at Barnsley to open 'a line of inland navigation between Sheffield, Rotherham, Barnsley, Wakefield, Leeds, Huddersfield, Manchester and Liverpool'. York and Beverley enjoyed a new prosperity as traffic increased on the Ouse and the Hull. The Don joined the Ouse, the Aire and the Calder at Goole, and the Trent at Keadby in Lincolnshire. In the agricultural East Riding, Driffield and Market Weighton gained access to the Humber, Pocklington to the Derwent. Canals breached even the great barrier of the Pennines: from Manchester via Rochdale came a spectacular stretch with 92 locks to join the Calder and Hebble at Sowerby Bridge; from Huddersfield to Ashton-under-Lyne went another through the Standedge Tunnel, 5,415 yards long, where men 'legged' barges from end to end, lying on their backs and walking along the roof. ('To leg a boat through such a distance,' assures one practical canal authority, 'calls for a unique and demanding posture, as well as stamina of the highest order.') Most famous of all, perhaps, was the Leeds and Liverpool Canal, 130 miles long and 46 years in the building, though once completed, by contemporary account, it 'enriched Ormskirk, Wigan, Blackburn, Burnley and Colne, in Lancashire, and Skipton, Keighley, Bingley, and Bradford, in Yorkshire'. Engineer James Brindley preferred long level stretches and steep flights of locks, and notably in his eight Bingley locks produced one of the wonders of the canal age.

Understandably, the times demanded a more precise sense of geography. The imaginative cartography of Saxton and his successors had compensated for a lack of detail with an artistic use of coats of arms, spouting sea-monsters and hills like puddings; roads had been ignored, their approximate courses suggested only by the inclusion of bridges (Defoe showed a similar pre-occupation with bridges rather than roads). With the Restoration came John Ogilby and his surveyors, walking the highways

42 *Plan of Bradford, about 1770*

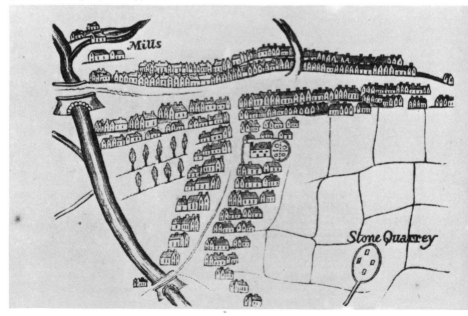

pushing their measuring wheels and producing a set of strip maps which sketched the passage of each road through 'arrable' and 'moorish ground', denoting landmarks in the form of windmills, 'colepits', even gallows. In 1720 John Warburton, a Bedale Supervisor of Excise, published 'A New and Correct Map of the County of York', intended only for 'persons of distinction' who had subscribed to have their arms included. Warburton employed sundry 'ingenious young men' to trundle his measuring wheel and climb church towers to take bearings, but his work marked a development insofar as it combined Saxton's background and Ogilby's roads, with others he had himself surveyed. But eighteenth-century cartography took its greatest stride forward with the magnificent inch-to-the-mile atlas of Yorkshire maps surveyed between 1767 and 1770 by Thomas Jefferys, Geographer to King George III: his fine engraving represented the very shape of the hills and drew a distinction between turnpike and other roads, and he incorporated such increasingly important features as lead, iron and coal mines, the Ripon Navigation and the intended Leeds and Liverpool Canal. A lucid idea of landscape was emerging.

It was a landscape undergoing drastic change. The age-old agriculture whereby a farmer's holdings were distributed in strips about rotating open fields, while his livestock grazed on common lands, had been gradually whittling away by enclosure for several centuries. But now, in tune with the period, the process was accelerated. New roads were disrupting the isolation of villages no longer of necessity self-sufficient, and whose farming methods must meet the growing demands of hungry rising towns. Hence, enclosure proceeded apace as the more substantial landowners sought Acts of Parliament to redistribute their holdings into larger, fewer and ultimately more productive units denoted by walls or hedges—to this movement belong many of the distinctive stone walls of the Pennines. At the same time they enclosed sizeable areas of common land, sometimes misleadingly referred to as 'waste' but in reality the communal source of peat, wood and scratch grazing for the poor who, now dispossessed, tended to hire out as labourers for their larger neighbours or to move into the expanding towns. A natural process thereby left a taste of equally natural resentment, which in Yorkshire found its proletarian voice in the anonymous author of *Snaith Marsh*, written in

1754:

But far more waeful still that luckless day
Which with the commons gave Snaith Marsh away;
Snaith Marsh our whole town's pride, the poor man's bread,
Where tho' no rent he paid, his cattle fed,
Fed on the sweetest grass which here rife grew,
Common to all, nor fence nor landmark knew.

Poetic license has romanticized this picture of pre-enclosure days: eighteenth-century reclamation was more often of land neglected, worn-out, over-grazed. 'Every plan of improving the general state and surface of the country, either by Enclosure, Drainage, Building, or Navigation, found in him an active friend and supporter,' declares an 1801 monument to one 'enlightened country gentleman', Sir Christopher Sykes of Sledmere. 'Whoever now traverses the Wolds of Yorkshire, and contrasts their present appearance with what they were, cannot but extol the name of Sykes.' William Marshall, contemporary writer on rural economy, was impressed by the 'SPIRIT OF IMPROVEMENT' (the capitals are his) which he found in the East Riding.

With improving land came fresh farming methods, better ploughs, new seed-drills, harrows, threshing machines, use of manure. Horses were superseding oxen for hauling and ploughing, though not everybody welcomed the change. 'An ox which I worked several years might, at seventeen or eighteen years old, have challenged, for strength, agility and sagacity, the best bred cart horse in the kingdom,' quoth Marshall, who thought a popular breed of 'black fen horses' more suitable for eating than for working. Reports to the Board of Agriculture detailed a countryside groping towards scientific advance. Attention was belatedly paid to the quality of livestock, though it was not unusual for a sheep-farmer to run three or four breeds together, whilst the appearance of Swaledale sheep still suggested that 'considerable pains had been taken to select the refuse of the several counties from which they have been brought'. New crops were being introduced, sometimes for surprising reasons: turnips, for winter fodder; carrots, for fattening pigs; cabbages, for feeding cattle — rural journalist Arthur Young, in 1770, watched Cleveland milch cows eating cabbages 'with great eagerness'; whereupon their

43   Brimham Rocks, with two gentlemen measuring

yield increased but the milk tasted of cabbage! Turnips grown in fields still open, another writer noted, were no bigger than an egg; and indeed, contemporary economists were unanimous in their view of the superiority of enclosed agriculture. In the Vale of Pickering, open land was let for 2*s* 6*d* to 4*s* per acre; enclosed, from 7*s* to 10*s* per acre.

If enlightened Georgian gentlemen can be said to have pulled agriculture out of the Middle Ages into comparatively modern times, they also awoke to an appreciation of natural beauty. To be sure, they preferred the picture-framed niceness of a well-ordered landscape. 'After the eye had traversed over a rich and fertile vale,' flows a typical measured description, near the Westmorland border in 1781, 'variegated with woods and country houses, the prospect was terminated with a chain of lofty mountains, which run in a direction from south to north, parallel to the course of the river'; some water-mills added 'an agreeable variety' to the scene. But those same Nature-lovers were also experiencing delicious thrills at Yorkshire's less regulated aspects: high Ingleborough, 'whose head was wrapt in a cloud'; the black rocks of Kingsdale (though 'a Mr Tomlinson, at Burton in Lonsdale', was making 'elegant monuments' out of them); wind-eroded Brimham Rocks in Nidderdale, 'astonishing, noble', and pronounced 'standing miracles'; those 'most stupendous' precipices of Malham Cove and Gordale Scar; and the West Riding's abundance of 'horrid' caves and potholes. Into the latter, indeed, ventured parties of scholarly sightseers equipped with guides, bundles of candles and baskets of provisions, to be inevitably reminded of classical legends, Stygian lakes and Aeneas entering the infernal regions. 'From the roof,' wrote John Hutton, wonder-struck chronicler of such early expeditions, 'were pendent large petrifactions in every grotesque shape; some like hams, others like neat's tongues, many like the heads and various parts of different animals. As we proceeded along we met with several bye streets or lanes, down some of which came tinkling little currents; but they seemed not to admit a passenger with ease to any great distance.' After 70 yards of this investigation, however, 'we had no curiosity to explore any farther'.

A growing love of holiday travel and the leisured classes' quest for health led to the steady rise of Yorkshire spas. Harrogate's waters increased in scope and variety: to its chalybeate springs

44   *The New Sulphur Spring, Harrogate*

in use since the sixteenth century were added a Sulphur Well
('the sulphurous impregnation renders it extremely nauseous at
first') for scrofula and worms, the so-called Cheltenham Water,
'a gentle purgative', the Tewit Well with its milky taste 'particularly useful in cases of the gravel', and the Crescent Well, discovered
in 1783 and surmounted by a cupola, a subscription to which was
'half-a-guinea for the season'. Leeds proved the slightly unexpected
setting for 'several remarkable springs' of benefit to rheumatic
sufferers and those with sore eyes—who could also obtain relief
through water from Roseberry Topping. Scarborough catered
for the fashion in bathing—likewise recommended for reasons of
health rather than enjoyment—men being rowed out to sea then
jumping in naked, women demurely submerging clad in gowns.
'There are thirty-six machines for sea-bathing,' counted one
visitor, a gentleman aged 80 who boasted he could still walk—
'with ease'—30 miles a day. 'I have often observed eight or ten in
the water at the same time . . . The bathers are fond of a full tide;
but I can see no evil in bathing at low water, except the length of
the way; for, as no river runs into the sea to weaken it, the water
at all times must have the same effect.' This writer revealed that
Scarborough natives scornfully nicknamed their visitors 'spaws'

and charged them 7*s* 6*d* to taste the waters, but at any rate they cured his daughter's asthma; he also recorded a proposed race between a Yorkshireman and a Lancastrian, 'to run eight miles upon the sands, for one hundred guineas, though many hundreds in bets were depending' (this was cancelled because of the Yorkshireman's non-appearance at the appointed time).

The Georgian populace well knew how to amuse themselves, their pleasures, unlike those of previous generations, virtually uncurtailed by civil wars and upheavals. The Jacobite Rebellion of 1745 barely brushed the county in its passing, though loyal citizens were thrown into consternation, some hiding their valuables and driving their stock into less accessible corners. One Arthur Jessop, a Holmfirth apothecary and diarist, kept a panicky day-by-day record of rumours and amateur military undertakings: of the chief constable coming round collecting money 'to raise men against the Rebels'; of sermons 'to animate us to stand for King & Country'; of Mr Eden, the local Presbyterian minister, officering a private army for home defence, the men arming themselves with 'Iron forks &c'—with which, mercifully, they were not called upon to join battle. At any rate, Yorkshire raised a volunteer Royal Regiment of Hunters, York itself four companies called the Blues 'for the safeguard of the city'; whilst Leeds stood host to a sizeable government army. Doncaster complained about the number of sick redcoats quartered on the town, chiefly because many were foreign mercenaries; but the grateful Quakers of the region redressed the balance by giving flannel waistcoats to the soldiers marching north after the retreating Scots. Throughout, there was a lively searching out of alleged rebel spies, and 22 Jacobites were executed at York in 1746, two of their heads being, by hallowed tradition, exhibited on Micklegate Bar.

Crowds eager, then, for entertainment gathered at any excuse. To older sports of foot-racing, cock-fighting, bull-baiting (a bull at Birstall once broke loose and drove some of his tormentors into a pond) was added the gentler cricket. Horse-racing grew fashionable—'there is scarce a village so mean,' observed a historian of 1736, 'that has not a bit of plate raised once a year for the purpose': Yorkshire boasted 40 race-courses. Public hangings reached a new peak of popularity; when highwayman Dick Turpin was turned off at York in 1739, he posthumously provided several days' amusement as mobs of residents, mourners and 'resurrection-men' fought and intrigued for possession of his corpse. Body-snatching, incidentally, long a source of worry to the bereaved and of benefit to the medical profession, was to reach its peak in the early decades of the following century, by which time improving communications facilitated the transfer of numerous Yorkshire cadavers to the dissecting-rooms of Edinburgh. A suicide buried at East Ardsley would reappear in a package aboard a coach at Leeds; a dead woman and child would arrive at Manchester in a box labelled 'To the Rev. Mr Gcneste, Hull, per Selby packet. To be left until called for. Glass, and keep this side up . . .' Not until the Anatomy Act of 1832, with its legalizing of the individual's right to 'direct that his body after death be examined anatomically', would the grave-robber or 'resurrection-man', equipped with his spade and crowbar and sack, relinquish his unsavoury role.

Meanwhile, a genre of dashing showmen proved anxious to supply ingenious diversions. In 1720 one Robertson presented himself before 5,000 spectators and the magistrates at Leeds, and took out of his folded handkerchief a tiny leathern boat in which, having inflated it with a pair of bellows, he 'swam upon the river Aire'. Thomas Pelling, a self-styled 'flying man', less successful, died after descending too rapidly from the pinnacle of Pocklington church in 1733. Foster Powell, a Horsforth pedestrian, specialized in walking from York to London and back: his record time for the return trip was five days 13 hours and 15 minutes, not markedly slower than by coach. And in 1786 Vicenzo Lunardi, England's first aeronaut, was cheered rapturously up in his balloon from both York and Leeds. . . .

Into this climate burst the mid-century religious revival, offering its evangelical fervour as alternative to the dry ministrations of a Church of England grown largely colourless and unexciting. It was a happy inspiration which led George Whitefield, barred from the pulpit at Bristol in 1739, to preach in the open air, as it was natural that the resultant emotional sense of occasion should attract substantially the common folk. John Nelson, a Birstall stone-mason converted by John Wesley, introduced Methodism to Yorkshire in 1741, and Wesley, on his first visit to the county the following year, appropriately preached at Birstall to 'several hundreds of plain people' on top of a hill, thereby setting the pattern for revivalist meetings: at Leeds he 'cried to

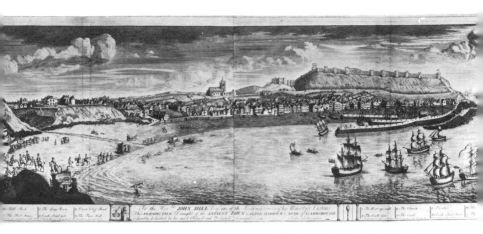

45   *Panoramic eighteenth-century view of 'the ancient town, castle, harbour and spa of Scarborough'*

thousands', and at Huddersfield the 'wildest congregation' he had seen in Yorkshire was induced to listen and feel 'the sharpness of His word'. Others found the gift of holding outdoor audiences: 'My church began to be crowded, insomuch that many were obliged to stand out of doors,' wrote the Rev. William Grimshaw, Anglican perpetual curate of Haworth yet a strong supporter of Yorkshire Methodism. 'Here, as in other places, it was amazing to hear and see what weeping, roaring, and agonies many people were seized with at the apprehension of their sinful state, and the wrath of God.' His church served a moorland township not easy of access, and could cram in 1,000 hearers—yet Grimshaw was sometimes obliged to preach to growing crowds in the churchyard. A combination of Whitefield and Grimshaw at Haworth communion services in 1753 witnessed the 'sipping away' of 35 bottles of wine.

Early revivalism owed much to the extrovert personality and showman's eye of its preachers: 'For shame! For shame!' Grimshaw once admonished a pew-holder before announcing his text. 'Don't you see that old woman standing there in the aisle ready to drop? Open the pew door and let her in!' Or again, mounting an outside scaffold to find a pillow serving as Bible-rest, he flung it into the crowd with a 'What! Do you think we come here to sleep!' But Methodism's sure hold, especially on the poorer classes, was soon indicated by a growing number of chapels —Wesley thought an octagonal one at Yarm, on the south bank of the Tees, 'by far the most elegant in England'—and by the 1760s an estimated third of the country's Methodists lived in Yorkshire. Others, too, swelled the Nonconformist ranks. The no less forceful Benjamin Ingham of Ossett established a chain of meeting-houses in the industrializing North, and in 1746 the Moravians, a Protestant sect originating in Bohemia and reaching Yorkshire by way of America where both Wesley and Ingham had met their missionaries, founded their settlement at Fulneck, near Pudsey. 'The aim in erecting this village,' they declared, 'was, that we might dwell together in true fellowship of the faith, in brotherly love and simplicity of heart under the direction of the only head of the church, our Lord Jesus Christ.' The community framed rules conducive to 'a quiet and peaceable life in all godliness and honesty'; built its own church, houses, schools and shop; provided its own employment, cloth-weaving, tailoring, glove and shoe-making for its Brethren, spinning, needlework and hosiery for its Sisters; and enlivened its daily round with a diversity of love-feasts, foot-washings, and blowing of trumpets in cemeteries at Easter dawns, watched by a credulous 'multitude of Strangers' who, not grasping the symbolism, half-expected the Moravians to raise the dead.

The eighteenth century exhibited the most obvious contrasts: ignorance and culture, rich and poor, cruelty and enlightenment. Many social features destined for indispensability were making a tentative beginning. Yorkshire's first newspaper, the *Leeds Mercury*, appeared in 1718, boasting 'the freshest advices, Foreign and Domestick', but containing as yet no local news; to be closely followed by the *York Mercury* and, in the next few decades, by the *York Courant*, the *Hull Courant*, the *Leeds Intelligencer*, the *Sheffield Weekly Journal*, the *Halifax Advertiser* . . . Gentlemen found a venue for reading and discussing them in the coffee-houses, a trifle more genteel than ale-houses but not so rarified as the voguish assembly-rooms, the atmosphere of which is tellingly suggested by a frequenter's description of those at York: 'Here the significant glance is seen, and the language of the eyes well understood. Here the gentle squeeze of the hand revives the heart; fashions are scrutinized, and reputations a little fractured. Here the seeds of love are sown, which grow to maturity, and shed their influence on the generations to come.'

Halifax and Leeds led the field in opening subscription libraries in 1768, the latter so enthusiastically received that it subsequently moved into what one contemporary scholar called 'a splendid apartment which would not disgrace a college'; others were started at Sheffield in 1771, Bradford in 1774, Hull and Whitby in 1775. No longer was reading confined to lofty edification, the English novel being mightily advanced by that humorous parson of Coxwold, the Rev. Laurence Sterne, whose *Tristram Shandy* became 'the talk of London and Paris'. The theatre was raised from the level of rumbustious public-house entertainment to fulfil a more artistic role, complete with 'improved' versions of Shakespeare and performing dogs in the intervals—Tate Wilkinson, managing a circuit based on the York Theatre Royal, rewrote *Hamlet* with a happy ending. For years a tragedian called Bridge Frodsham, rejoicing in the soubriquet 'the York Roscius', reigned as stage idol; once, on a trip to London, he called on Garrick, whom he baffled with his 'self-sufficient airs', declaring that he had 'come there merely to see a few plays, and visit a brother genius'. Samuel Butler, actor-manager of a North and East Riding circuit, built Yorkshire's most notable 'proper theatre' of all in 1788, at Richmond, then a fashionable Swaledale centre, its quiet elegance and Doric pillars reflecting in miniature the architecture of its day.

Indeed, Yorkshire helped set the style of the age. Epitome of the gifted patron was Richard Boyle, 3rd Earl of Burlington and architect of the York assembly-rooms, magnificently if tenuously based on the sixteenth-century Italian Palladio's designs of a reconstructed Egyptian house described by the ancient Roman architect Vitruvius: this started a whole craze in Egyptian halls. Under Burlington's influence, another versatile Yorkshireman, William Kent, turned from painting to architecture and was responsible for much of London's Georgian building. At a time when stately homes were growing statelier, John Carr of Horbury prolifically helped grace both townscape and landscape, his designs ranging from Harewood House and Kirkleatham Hall to Leeds Infirmary, York County Lunatic Asylum, the County Assize Courts and the grandstand at Knavesmire race-course. In a smaller compass, Thomas Chippendale of Otley perfected his exquisite furniture from mixed French, Chinese and Gothic models.

The eighteenth century enjoyed a prodigal inventiveness and

46   The elegance of eighteenth-century York: the Debtors' Prison (1701–1705), and, on the right, the Assize Courts (1773–1777)

initiative in many fields. From Whitby sailed the great whaling captain, William Scoresby, returning from his voyage of 1797 with 16 whales yielding 152 tuns of oil, 'more than had before entered the port of Whitby in any one ship'. Originator of such evocative seafaring techniques as the posting of masthead lookouts in the 'top-gallant crow's nest', and freeing a vessel from ice by sallying or having its crew run from side to side across the deck, Scoresby brought home from his 30 expeditions a total of 533 whales, together with 'many thousands of seals, some hundreds of walruses, very many narwals, and probably not less than sixty bears'. From Whitby, too, sailed James Cook, a Cleveland grocer's boy with the sea in his blood: the first ship he sailed in was the coastal collier *Freelove*; and when in 1768 he commanded the Royal Society's expedition to the South Seas, he chose for the venture a hardy, shallow-draught collier brig built at Whitby and renamed the *Endeavour*, which thereby voyaged far indeed from familiar waters to chart the way to the Society Islands, New Zealand and Australia. Again, in 1759 a gold ball was screwed on top of the cupola of a new Eddystone lighthouse by civil engineer John Smeaton, who as a lad had made model pumps and windmills at Whitkirk outside Leeds. Meanwhile, an unorthodox

Birstall theologian, Joseph Priestley, was experimenting with electricity, fermentation, respiration, oxygen. . . .

But there was another side to the coin. Parliamentary representation remained essentially unchanged since the thirteenth century, and the whole of Yorkshire returned just 30 Members: two Knights of the Shire or county, and two each from 14 ancient boroughs. Some of the latter were 'pocket boroughs' controlled by local nobility or patrons, others were 'rotten' and elected whichever candidate paid high enough; whilst voting rights based on land tenure and building rents ensured a small and usually manageable number of electors. Hence, the Duke of Newcastle could call Boroughbridge and Aldborough 'my own two boroughs' and pick their four Members; the Duke of Devonshire owned all 84 houses carrying voters' rights at Knaresborough; the Dundas family held Richmond, the Lascelles Northallerton. The 300 electors of Hedon, on the other hand, chose the candidate who paid them. York, with some 2,500 voters, and Hull with 1,600, were less easily dictated to, but for some years Hull candidates rewarded 'the poorer order of voters' to the tune of two guineas a vote, the bribe being regarded as 'a sort of birthright'. At Pontefract in 1768 when independent-minded electors, galled at the official candidates' refusal to feast them in the customary way, ventured to run their own rival nominee, the town was given up to riot and intimidation. Not even the size of the county itself, with 25,000 voters, assured its freedom of candidate; the expenses of contesting an election were so great that Whigs and Tories usually agreed to choose an unopposed Member each. On the one occasion, in

47 *Whitby*

1807, when an election was fought, it cost an estimated £250,000. Meanwhile, developing towns as important as Leeds, Halifax and Sheffield had no Parliamentary representation. Petitions for reform went unheeded, and at Sheffield a Society for Constitutional Information took to celebrating French Revolutionary victories with a show of Republican flags.

The working classes, then, had no legitimate outlet for expressing their grievances and, insecure in this century of social change and rising populations, were frequently excited into disorders exacerbated by their confrontations with the troops who were usually called out against them. At Leeds, as we have seen, there was rioting against the turnpikes. Similarly, the enclosure of Stannington and Hallam commons sparked off a rising at Sheffield in 1791, in which the gaol was broken into, the vicarage damaged and hay-ricks burned. The poor interpreted the Militia Act of 1757 as compelling them to defend the property of the rich, and reacted with widespread upheavals: at York a 'vast body' of farmers, artisans and labourers demolished the deputy-lieutenants' meeting-house. A 'most outrageous' riot at Beeston in 1797 indicated the shape of things to come, when workers suspicious of new machinery destroyed a cloth-mill. But the recurring theme was the most vital one of all, namely the state of harvests and the cost of corn. At Leeds in 1735, soldiers fired on a bread mob, killing several. Five years later, in four days of rioting round Wakefield and Dewsbury, waggons of meal and mills were attacked. The 1790s brought especial hardship and frequent outbreaks in the manufacturing districts—a Castleford mob described at the time as 'starving' seized a boat-load of corn, giving it up only after the reading of the Riot Act and the appearance of the military.

The lot of the poor could be hard indeed. At Bradford in 1796, with wheat selling at 17s a bushel, they lived on a scanty fare of barley, bean and pea meal; five years later the sterner sort at Leeds determined not to eat more than one loaf per family per week till the price should have come down to 10s a bushel. Ecclesfield labourers existed substantially on 'water-pottage', consisting of boiling water, oatmeal and onions, with butter, but 'the proportions of oatmeal and butter,' observed a commentator in 1795, 'have been much lessened since the rise in the price of those articles' (which leaves boiling water and onions). Some were reduced to eating nettles, 'which they boil, and season with a little salt and pepper'. Over-stretched parishes, responsible for the relief of their own poor, passed vagrants and strange paupers from one to another, each anxious to keep its rates down: two adults and a child died of exposure in transit on an open cart at Doncaster, and Crow Hill, on the Yorkshire-Lancashire border, retains a feasible legend of a wandering boy dead on the moor-top, unwanted by either side. Towards the end of the century, by which time the war with France was affecting trade, pushing up prices, and drawing off able-bodied men into the Army and Navy, Hull (where the press-gangs were active) carried the staggering total of 900 families in need, with 284 paupers in its workhouse. At Halifax, 180 out of 1,700 families required relief. Out-relief took the form of goods and money intended to help the needy struggle on in their own homes, and the accounts of Yorkshire Overseers of the Poor offer incidental evidence of a cottage industry: 'Ordered that James Judson be allowed 2s per week . . . that Rachel Green have cotton for a shift . . . that John Wright be allowed a double truss & 7s 6d towards fitting up a pair of looms . . . that John Waring have cloth allowed for a shirt . . . that Marshall's Child be allowed 20s towards a pair of looms as soon as it begins to weave . . .'

But parish workhouses provided a last resort for a sorry mixture of incompatibles. The 74 inmates at Bradford, during the 1790s, comprised 'mostly women, old men, and children; including six bastards, and as many lunatics'; Sheffield housed a motley collection of 'old and infirm, lunatics, soldiers' wives, or young children'; of 89 paupers at Halifax, 42 were under the age of 12, 20 under six, and a third of them were 'lunatic'. An average ten births a year in the Hull Charity Hall were 'almost entirely of bastards of young unmarried girls, sent into the house to lie-in'. At thrifty Sheffield, it was recorded, 'the old people dine first: what they leave, forms part of the dinner of the children'. The inmates of workhouses were intended (as the name implies) to work, but for obvious reasons this was not always practicable. A few spun worsted and lint at Ecclesfield, and the older paupers in Hull Charity Hall, one of the better-run establishments, were encouraged to 'teaze rope into oakum, for the use of ship-carpenters'. Some Sheffield inmates spun 'wool and lint, for stockings, shirts, sheets, and other articles for the use of the house'; whilst able-bodied men at Halifax went out to jobs in the town and were rewarded with butcher's meat for dinner every day.

The workhouse standard of living varied according to the parish. At Ecclesfield there were five or six beds to a room, and two or three paupers to a bed; Sheffield had generally only two beds to a room, but as many as four paupers slept in one bed; Leeds beds were crowded 20 to a room, and the bedclothes were scoured once a year. The diet tended to be better than that of many struggling along in the outside world: inmates of the Stokesley poor-house had milk and oatmeal every breakfast and supper, and a varied bill of fare for dinner, according to the day of the week—beef, roots and dumplings; potatoes, butter and fish; frumenty; fry and potatoes. There was broth and bread for supper at Leeds, Hull and Sheffield; two pints of beer at Halifax; and, at Sheffield, cheese, bread and beer on Saturdays. Christmas, Easter and Whitsuntide brought treats in the shape of spiced cake and plum-pudding; and in Halifax workhouse (lest our conception of such institutions should be too inhumanly forbidding) 'those who have been used to tobacco, are allowed ½ a lb a month; snuff-takers receive ½ a lb of snuff every month'!

FURTHER READING

Chapter 6
Frank Baker: William Grimshaw, 1708–1763, 1963.
H. B. Browne, M.A.: Chapters of Whitby History, 1946.
Bill Cowley: Farming in Yorkshire: a Regional Survey, 1972.
W. B. Crump: Huddersfield Highways Down the Ages, 1949.
Daniel Defoe: A Tour through England and Wales, Divided into Circuits or Journies, edited by G. D. H. Cole, 1927.
B. F. Duckham: Navigable Rivers of Yorkshire: their History and Traditions, 1964.
Sir Frederic Morton Eden: The State of the Poor, 1797.
John Hutton: A Tour to the Caves, in the Environs of Ingleborough and Settle, in the West-Riding of Yorkshire, 1781.
W. Hutton: A Tour to Scarborough in 1803, 1817.
The Diary of Arthur Jessop, edited by C. E. Whiting, D.D., F.S.A. (The Yorkshire Archaeological Society Record Series, Vol. CXVII), 1952.
David and Vanessa Neave: Georgian Yorkshire, 1971.

John E. Rawnsley, F.R.S.A.: *Antique Maps of Yorkshire and their Makers*, 1970.

Arthur Raistrick: *Yorkshire Maps and Map-Makers*, 1969.

48   *Mechanisation: the spinning machines of Arkwright, Hargreaves and Crompton*

7
The Industrial Revolution

The latter half of the eighteenth century was characterized by a series of inventions destined to take the cottagers and small masters witnessed by Defoe out of their homely if industrious surroundings, and to plant them in a harsher system epitomised by the West Riding's 'dark, satanic mills'. In 1733 John Kay, of Bury in Lancashire, had patented his flying shuttle which accelerated the process of hand-weaving. For centuries it had taken five spinners to keep one weaver supplied with yarn: now the ratio was stretched still further, till 1764 when James Hargreaves, of Blackburn, invented his spinning-jenny and so multiplied the spinners' output. Richard Arkwright and Samuel Crompton, again both Lancashire men, made additional improvements and their frames, at first hand-worked, were being driven by water-power in the 1770s. Meanwhile, James Watt was adapting Thomas Newcomen's steam engine, from a role limited to pumping water out of mines, to the driving of machinery; and in 1787 Edmund Cartwright, an inventive clergyman from Nottinghamshire, set up his first power-loom at Doncaster (its original motive-power was provided by a bull), and gradually steam replaced water as a means of power. Other developments included Arkwright's carding machine, transforming a process that had hitherto involved simply a child brushing wool or cotton from hand to hand to tease it out; and the cropping-frame of Enoch Taylor. a Marsden blacksmith, which was capable of doing the work of ten skilled hand-croppers. Cartwright also invented a woolcombing machine, nicknamed Big Ben after a notable prize-fighter of the day—his Doncaster workers had a rhyme beginning:

49 *Goose Eye, A West Riding hamlet of the Industrial Revolution: mill and workers' cottages huddled amongst the hilly fields. The chimney provides an obvious focal-point*

> *Come all ye master combers, and hear of our Big Ben,*
> *He'll comb more wool in one day than fifty of your men,*
> *With their hand-combs and comb-pots, and such old-fashioned ways;*
> *There'll be no more occasion for old Bishop Blaize . . .*

—the latter being the patron saint of hand-woolcombers.

The outcome of this mechanisation was inevitable: accelerating means of production strained the old system whereby clothiers had collected their pieces from cottage-bound weavers and sold them to merchants in the town markets; such limitations were overcome by concentrating workers in factories. Most inventions originated, it will be noted, in Lancashire, which consequently industrialised rather earlier than Yorkshire, where machinery meant for cotton had to be adapted to wool (though trade recognised no county boundaries, and some early cotton mills were in fact situated on the Yorkshire side of the Pennines: of 12 steam engines introduced into Yorkshire between 1785 and 1795, five were in cotton mills). In 1792 Benjamin Gott, a Leeds cloth merchant turned manufacturer, commenced building his Bean Ing woollen mill, with the dream of concentrating all the processes, from washing the raw wool to dyeing the finished product, under one roof; the River Aire supplied the necessary power, although his early weaving was done on handlooms and his spinning by hand-jennies. Another Leeds pioneer, John Marshall, installed four of Cartwright's power-looms in his flax mill as early as 1788, and by 1796 Arthur Young was noting the presence of six or seven steam engines in Leeds factories. An attempt to bring steam-power to Bradford in 1794 was scotched by residents who threatened: 'If you shall presume to erect any steam engine for the manufacture of cotton or wool we shall, if the same be found a nuisance, seek such redress as the law shall give'; so it was another four years before Bradford's first 15-horse-power mill-engine was set up in the Holme. By the opening decades of the new century, Leeds was being hailed as 'the principal seat of the Woollen Manufacture in England'; Bradford as a town thriving on a staple worsted trade.

The industrialisation of the West Riding was vastly encouraged by the coal measures conveniently extending from the Aire valley southwards through Sheffield into Derbyshire. Earlier transport difficulties had restricted the use of coal—though there was a busy coastal trade from Northumberland to London—and mining had comprised a haphazard digging of shallow tunnels and pits. But now, canals and better roads, together with improved pumping equipment, coincided with demands for coal to feed the new steam engines and fulfil the even more voracious needs of the iron and steel industry. Since the Roman occupation, charcoal had been

50   *West Riding clothiers on their way to market*

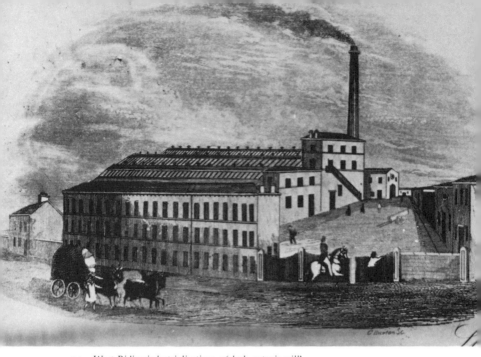

used for smelting iron, and a process whereby the production of a single ton of iron required a ton and a half of charcoal, had drastically reduced available timber. By the eighteenth century, the Sheffield region was importing bar iron from Sweden, though nearby Ecclesall Woods were dotted yet awhile with the cabins and smoking sod-covered woodstacks of charcoal-burners who lit their fires on Sundays in order to guarantee a supply for the steelworks by Saturday. Then, in Shropshire, Abraham Darby introduced coke into foundry-work, and a lengthy series of modifications and advances resulted in the employment of coal in the manufacture of iron and steel. The developing pattern was similar to that of the textile industry: small forges perched up the valleys, their bellows worked by waterwheels, moved down to where the coal was accessible, concentrating round Sheffield and Rotherham. The Masborough Ironworks, founded by a self-taught schoolmaster called Samual Walker, rose to become reputedly the biggest in Europe, thanks in part to the Napoleonic and American wars, for which they made 'immense quantities of cannon of the largest calibre'; more peaceably, they developed a speciality in cast-iron bridges. Farther north, a rather unexpected partnership of a clergyman, a solicitor and a country gentleman began—for it was an age of opportunity for those bold enough to take business risks—another famous ironworks in 1788 at Low Moor, near Bradford, which would grow into 'one of the most important industrial establishments in the world'.

The population had been steadily growing during the eighteenth century, Yorkshire as a whole doubling, and the West Riding trebling, their numbers. Steadily, under the influence of coal, of iron and steel and of textiles, as unsettled rural workers sought employment in towns, the West accelerated its lead over the North and East Ridings. Between 1801 and 1851, the West Riding population increased from 564,593 to 1,315,885, or much more than doubled; the East Riding went from 111,192 to 220,983, or rather less than doubled, though its 1851 total was still less than half that of the West Riding fifty years before; whilst the North Riding's 158,955 of 1801 had become only 215,225 by 1851. All the West Riding centres—Leeds, Sheffield, Halifax, Wakefield—and notably Hull in the East, doubled or more than trebled in size; Bradford spectacularly quintupled in the 40 years after 1801.

Such drastic growth met opposition from several quarters. A directory of 1822 irritably stressed how the more fastidious inhabitants of Bradford 'have of late years suffered considerable annoyance from the smoke emitted from steam engine furnaces'. Lovers of classical Georgian landscapes regretted their spoliation: Thomas Dunham Whitaker, chronicling the antiquities of Craven in the early 1800s and delighting in fittingly 'neat, healthful, and pleasant' villages, voiced outspoken disapproval of hitherto modest towns in process of expansion. A 'sudden increase' of population at Bingley seemed to him a circumstance 'which every moralist and every lover of his country must deplore'. At Keighley he respired 'the smoke of manufactories' and was 'stunned by the din of recent population'. In one sentence he crystallised both a scholar's romantic notion of the past and his shrewd predictions for a harsher future: 'Before the introduction of manufactories the parish of Kighley did not want its retired glens and well-wooded hills; but the clear mountain torrent now is defiled, its scaly inhabitants suffocated by filth, its murmurs lost in the din of machinery, and the native music of its overhanging groves exchanged for oaths and curses.'

Most vehement opponents of the changing order were, however, in many cases the workers themselves. A number of bad harvests, coinciding with the disruption of trade in the Napoleonic and American wars, brought high prices and unemployment and accentuated a situation wherein craftsmen felt their livelihoods jeopardised by mechanisation. At Nottingham, in 1811, hosiery weavers commenced smashing some new stocking-frames. Out of deference, it is thought, to an obscure writer of threatening letters signing himself 'Ned Ludd', machine-breakers in general took the name of Luddites, and their movement quickly spread to Yorkshire to find its chief exponents among the croppers.

Croppers, or shearmen, were a skilled class of craftsmen whose job it was to dress woollen cloth by using heavy hand-shears. They were well-paid, suspicious of machinery and jealous of their position: 20 years earlier they had successfully limited the use of gig-mills—machines for raising fibres on cloth preparatory to cropping—by striking, refusing to treat material which had passed through a gig-mill, and by resort to arson. Now they organised for battle against mechanising mill-owners, collecting weapons, levying funds, and forming secret societies (their taking of the necessary oath was engagingly called 'twissing in', because the swearer was being symbolically twisted into one fibre with his

52 *Croppers*

fellow-croppers). 1812 was a year of violence, particularly around Leeds and Huddersfield. Mills and workshops were attacked and frames broken by gangs of men with their faces blackened, wielding smiths' hammers nicknamed 'Enoch' after Enoch Taylor, who manufactured both cropping-frames and hammers—a circumstance from which the Luddites, quick to spot the irony, contrived their slogan: 'Enoch made them, Enoch shall break them.' They also had a song that lends a stirring lilt to an otherwise squalid episode:

> *Come, cropper lads of high renown,*
> *Who love to drink good ale that's brown,*
> *And strike each haughty tyrant down,*
> *With hatchet, pike, and gun!*
> *Oh, the cropper lads for me,*
> *The gallant lads for me,*
> *Who with lusty stroke,*
> *The shear frames broke,*
> *The cropper lads for me!*

Four thousand troops were called into the West Riding; citizens enrolled as special constables; mills were barricaded and guarded. Manufacturer William Horsfall, of Ottiwells Mills, Marsden, who had boasted that he would 'ride up to his saddle-girths' in Luddites' blood, was fatally shot from ambush riding home from Huddersfield market. But when the Luddites attempted a mass assault on Rawfolds Mill at Liversedge – a hated premises employing both shearing-frames and water-driven gig-mills— they met with a spirited resistance and left two dead and others wounded. Inevitably, their bitter struggle subsided in executions and transportations.

There were later, sporadic outbreaks of machine-smashing. In 1822 a Bradford worsted manufacturer smuggled an 'obnoxious' power-loom into a mill at Shipley, 'where he thought it would be safe', but the bellman spread news of its arrival and a mob of handloom weavers tore it to pieces. Four years later an attack on an Addingham mill was dispersed by the military (one rioter, trying to climb in along a ledge, fell into a privy cesspool and 'smothered'), and shots were exchanged between constables and some hundreds of unemployed throwing stones at weaving-mills in Bradford. 'The unfortunate operatives were, however, unable to obstruct the general adoption of the detested machines,' comments one observer, 'they were soon almost universally introduced into the manufactories.' Indeed, by 1835 more than 4,000 power-looms were in use in Yorkshire.

The factory system relied heavily and notoriously on the labour of women and children, though for many the mill was merely a more disciplined extension of their work in domestic industry. One John Kitson of Haworth, born 'of poor parents' in 1781, would leave a straightforward autobiography recording how his father 'went for a soldier when I was but a child so as I could not tell on him going', and how 'when I was about five years of age I began spinning worsted yarn and had five hanks set for my work a day'—the quota was raised by a hank each year, and obviously helped maintain a small-scale cottage system. 'But there was one called Blakey that took a mill at Bridgehouse and span cotton, and I began to go there when I was about seven years of age and tented five pair of cards near three years. Then I left there and went to a mill called Wright's mill to work near three years in the night, then they took me out to make up twist and I did that near two years . . .' By the time that lad was in his middle teens, he had been spinning, carding, twisting, weaving, working a night-shift, and had managed to lame himself; and the matter-of-fact style of his and similar reminiscences suggests that they were typical of very many.

The lot of the workers in the Industrial Revolution was notoriously hard: they worked unbelievably long hours while still very young, were beaten by their superiors, fined for being late . . . even allowing for a natural element of exaggeration, their own words speak graphically of their hardships. Some of the more literate expressed themselves in verse; Abraham Wildman, a young Keighley man, wrote touchingly on *The Factory Child's Complaint*:

> *Ere the lark salute the skies,*
> *Ere the sun upon us smile,*
> *From our wretched beds we rise,*
> *Weary with the last day's toil.*
>
> *Summoned by yon hateful bell,*
> *Morn and noon we're doomed to hear,*

Yes, it sounds like death's dull knell,
We, its victims of despair.

Other, simpler folk placed their experiences on record in the files of Select Committees investigating their conditions, as, for example, that under Michael Thomas Sadler, MP for Aldborough, seeking to regulate the hours of child labour in 1832. One Elizabeth Bentley testified that she had worked in a Leeds flax mill, at the age of six, from five o'clock in the morning till nine at night 'when they were thronged'. David Brook, a Leeds cloth-dresser, had worked for 36 hours without sleep, and David Bywater started at one o'clock one Monday morning and continued till five o'clock on Wednesday morning, his longest break being an hour and a half. A Stanningley tailor had three daughters in worsted mills from three in the morning till ten at night 'in the brisk time'.

Many factories, it seemed, allowed only 30 or 40 minutes for dinner, with no time off for 'breakfast or drinking'. 'We had to eat our meals,' said Joseph Hebergam, who had worked aged seven near Huddersfield, 'as we could; standing or otherwise.' Hannah Brown of Bradford had no time at all for meals, and Charles Burns at Leeds got 40 minutes for dinner, but was expected to clean the machinery, too. Matthew Crabtree, in a Dewsbury cotton mill, often found his food covered with flues; whilst Elizabeth Bentley's overlooker used to take home the children's uneaten dinners to feed his pigs. Both ends of the working day were a battle against sleep. Matthew Crabtree remembered his parents lifting him out of bed asleep, and Samuel Coulson and his wife often had to dress their three girls, who had been in bed for only three hours, at two o'clock in the morning. Joseph Firth of Keighley recalled how, as a child still working at ten at night, 'I was in such a state of stupor when I pieced an end, that I have had the skin taken off my fingers and hands; being asleep, as one may say, the frames went against my fingers.' He and his workmates would sit on the window-bottoms and fall asleep, 'and then the overlooker used to come and shake us by the ear, or give us a rap with the strap'. Punishment of children flagging with fatigue could be severe. 'There were three overlookers,' stated Joseph Hebergam of Huddersfield; 'there was a head overlooker, and there was one man kept to grease the machines, and

53   The factory system—clogs, shawls and child workers outside a West Riding mill

there was one kept on purpose to strap.'

The strap forms a recurring theme. Benjamin Bradshaw described it as 'a sort of leathern belt'. John Dawson's overlooker at Leeds 'kept a strap with a strong handle, and sometimes they struck with the handle, and sometimes with the leather part'. Generally, said William Hebden, they aimed for the small of the back or the head. At a Keighley worsted mill, when Samuel Rhodes was six, the overlooker 'had a strap with nails in it'. Once Robert Colton, working on occasion an 18-hour day at Bradford, had lain down on the floor worn out, and had been beaten with the strap. Jonathan Downe of Leeds had seen boys knocked down with it. Benjamin Gummersall had been strapped 'black and blue' at Bradford, and had his ears torn; Benjamin Fox had known children hit 'so bad as to make the blood stream down their heads', and one of Samuel Coulson's daughters had come home with her back 'beat nearly to a jelly'. Children were also kept awake, it transpired, by being jogged about, dowsed with cold water, or rapped over the head with bobbins. Hannah Brown had seen 'Mr Ackroyd' pull a relative of hers about by her hair, and at Gomersal, William Kershaw had been struck with a billy-roller till he had vomited blood—a billy-roller, incidentally, was 'perhaps two or three yards in length, and perhaps an inch and a half or more in diameter'.

Even the needs of nature were regulated. 'Were you allowed,' a Leeds 13-year-old was asked, 'to make water at any time that you

128

wanted?' He replied: 'No; only when a boy came to tell you it was your turn, and whether we wanted or not, that was the only time allowed us; if we did not go when he came round, we could not go at all.'

Under the circumstances, accidents were not uncommon. Joseph Hebergam knew of a boy who, 'to fettle the machine, was kneeling down, and a strap caught him about his ankles and carried him round the wheel, and dashed his brains out on the floor'. A Dewsbury girl had been pulled up to the ceiling; a Leeds girl had lost both arms; and Thomas Smith of Keighley had been caught by the upright shaft, his left arm broken in three places, 'and my head was sadly damaged'. Another Keighley man spoke of frequently seeing children 'without arms, without legs, and without fingers; and we can produce in Keighley 150 rickety, crooked-legged children, owing to their being overwrought'. The factory system bred unhealthy children, a pathetic number of Sadler's witnesses being requested to show the Committee their crippled limbs. 14-year-old William Kenworthy, from Huddersfield, was 'excessively deformed' in the legs and knees. James Carpenter had been crooked from the age of 12. Eliza Marshall, 17 years old, had an iron on her right leg, and the doctors at Leeds Infirmary had told her that 'the marrow is dried out of the bone, so that there is no natural strength in it'. Dwarfish, deformed Thomas Smith from Keighley had been sent home from a cotton mill at the age of six, because 'I was too little, I could not reach my work.' Once workers were crippled, there was little prospect for them. Elizabeth Bentley, a weigher in a Leeds card-room, was deformed at 13 and in the poor-house at 23. William Hebden, crooked at eight, eked out an existence selling potatoes. When Benjamin Gummersall grew bent, they gave him a stool and reduced his wage from 5s 6d to 4s 6d. Joseph Hebergam's brother and sister used to hold him by each arm and drag him to his Huddersfield mill, his poor legs trailing behind. 'Oh! if I had a thousand pounds,' he said, 'I would give them to have the use of my limbs again.'

Workers in Yorkshire's other industries fared equally badly. A Parliamentary report of 1843 presents a horrific portrait of grinders in Sheffield, who by the age of 20 were exhibiting 'the symptoms of their peculiar complaint . . . they stoop forward, and appear to breathe most comfortably in that position in

which they are accustomed to sit at their work, viz. with their elbows resting on their knee. Their complexion assumes a dirty, muddy appearance. Their countenance indicates anxiety; they complain of a sense of tightness across the chest . . . They occasionally expectorate considerable quantities of dust, sometimes mixed up with mucus . . .' Down coal-mines liable to floods and fire-damp explosions, women and children worked naked alongside men under what were generally called 'revolting' conditions that encouraged immorality. Said a Halifax pit-girl, whose job was to crawl on all fours pulling corves weighing three hundredweight by means of a belt round her waist and a chain between her legs: 'The boys take liberties with me sometimes; they pull me about.' She thought she would rather work in a mill than in a coal-pit.

Yet the gulf between masters and workers was not necessarily a wide one, in those earlier decades of industrialisation. Occasionally, everybody could meet on common ground, as in the February 3rd festivities in honour of Bishop Blaize, the patron saint of woolcombers. West Riding centres like Leeds and Bradford, Halifax and Doncaster, took turns to celebrate with special pomp every seventh year, with a holiday—'Hundreds go by here, I may say thousands,' grumbled a Bramley scribbling miller in 1811. 'Mill standing, all our men gone to Bradford'—much ale-drinking, and a pageant illustrative of the history and legend of wool. A spectacular procession at Bradford in 1825 included a motley army of woolstaplers, worsted spinners and manufacturers, merchants, woolsorters, charcoal-burners, comb-makers, combers and dyers, with flags and bands and fancy-dress representing Bishop Blaize, Jason and the Golden Fleece, shepherds and shepherdesses. 'The *blaze*,' punned the *Leeds Mercury* referring to accompanying bonfires, 'was not out in Bradford yesterday, though the *beer*-engines had been playing upon it ever since Monday.'

Then, too, many mill-owners were men of humble beginnings who often enjoyed more initiative than business sense or luck. A period of over-speculation and shaky finance backed by a proliferation of small private banks, crashing in 1826, ruined hundreds of manufacturers large and small, and would be fearfully remembered for the rest of the century as the Butterworth Panic, after a hapless Messrs Butterworth which was the first Yorkshire firm to fail. Again, the Combination Acts in force from 1799 to 1824 prohibited workers' unions as contrary to the public interest: the strikes which followed their repeal—notably those of the Bradford Union Association of Woolcombers and Stuff Weavers lasting 23 weeks in 1825, and the Saddleworth Weavers'

55   A Bishop Blaize procession: its characters include the Bishop, on horseback, shepherds and a shepherdess, and the Golden Fleece

Union in the winter of 1828—ended in bitter defeats for operatives not yet schooled in effective organisation.

Hence, it was left to social reformers and Members of Parliament to better the lot of the working classes, by protective legislation which came but slowly and tentatively. An Act of 1802 sought to 'preserve the health and morals' of pauper children drafted into factories, but its concern that apartments should be washed with quicklime and water twice a year and that 'not more than Two Apprentices shall sleep in the same Bed' was cautious in the extreme and almost impossible to enforce. Sir Robert Peel's Factory Act of 1819, suggesting a minimum working age of nine for children in cotton mills, and a maximum working day of 12 hours for nine- to 16-year-olds, was likewise, in default both of birth certificates and factory inspectors, virtually unenforceable. Weak Acts of 1825 and 1831 respectively introduced the idea of a part-holiday on Saturdays (working time limited to nine hours!) and prohibited night-shifts for those under 21.

But in 1830 Richard Oastler, born at Leeds, educated at the Fulneck Moravian school and now a steward at Fixby near Huddersfield, was talking to a Bradford worsted spinner about the West Indies slave trade, when the conversation turned to the factory system. 'I had lived for many years,' wrote Oastler, 'in the very heart of the factory districts; I had been on terms of intimacy and of friendship with many factory masters, and I had all the while fancied that factories were blessings to the poor.' Thus suddenly enlightened, his letter on 'Yorkshire Slavery' to the *Leeds Mercury* heralded a strenuous campaign for a ten-hour working day for women and children. Parliamentary leader in this cause was Michael Thomas Sadler, Member for Aldborough at the suggestion of the Duke of Newcastle whose 'rotten borough' it was. His hard work on the Select Committee of which he was chairman in 1832 possibly broke his health, and later that year the passing of the Reform Bill cost him his seat. Nevertheless, the Factory Act of 1833, if achieving less than he had hoped, instituted government inspection and factory schools, and set a maximum nine-hour day for children aged nine to 13. Eleven years later this minimum age was actually lowered to eight, but the maximum day reduced to 6½ hours. After Sadler, the Parliamentary lead was taken by Lord Ashley, later the Earl of Shaftesbury; but it was given to John Fielden in 1847 to steer the coveted Ten Hours

56 *Richard Oastler, 'The Factory King' (1789–1861)*

Act to fruition. Fielden was a Todmorden man, son of a yeoman turned small-scale cotton-spinner; as a boy he had worked in his father's mill, which subsequently he and his brothers built into one of the biggest cotton firms in the country; and in 1832 he was elected MP for Oldham. 'In the House of Commons,' relates his entry in the *Dictionary of National Biography*, 'he did not shine as an orator. His voice was very weak; he spoke with a strong provincial accent, and neither his elaborate industrial statistics nor the minute details of his descriptions of distress in the manufacturing districts were appreciated by the House.' Be that as it may, factory workers subscribed towards his statue at Todmorden in 1875. To Lord Ashley, meanwhile, went the credit for the Mines and Collieries Regulation Act of 1842, prohibiting the underground employment of women and boys less than 13 years old.

All the while, as the nineteenth century advanced, the pace of the West Riding's industry quickened. As early as 1758, Middleton Colliery, near Leeds, had run its horse-drawn coal-waggons along a mile and a half of tramway across Hunslet Moor to the Old Staith on the Aire. The next step was to replace the horses by a stationary steam engine pulling waggons by drawing in a cable; and the next after that, a movable or 'locomotive' steam engine

57　*Christ Church, Leeds, with the Middleton steam locomotive*

driven by means of cogs fitting into a toothed rail. This, the patent of John Blenkinsop of the same colliery and christened the *Prince Regent*, began hauling coals in 1812, and could pull eight (one awe-struck account credits 30) laden waggons at a speed of 3½ miles an hour. It and its sister engine, the *Salamanca*, became 'one of the principal curiosities of the neighbourhood'; even the Grand Duke and future Tsar Nicholas of Russia came to watch them, voicing 'expressions of no slight admiration'. Another and more pertinent visitor was engineer George Stephenson; and though his Stockton to Darlington line is not directly part of Yorkshire's story, its promoters met in the George and Dragon Inn at Yarm, to which a short branch line opened in 1825 became the first public railway in the county. Though railway development would not get into its full stride until approaching mid-century, improving communications were soon encouraging the growth of trade. The textile regions enjoyed an outlet to America by way of the Leeds and Liverpool Canal; whilst Hull, linked by rail through Selby and Leeds to the West Riding in 1840 and steadily expanding its docks, was in process of becoming Britain's third seaport, exporting coal and manufactures, importing wool from Australia, pit props from the Baltic, iron from Sweden and Russia. As its whaling industry declined, ship-building and fishing grew.

Manufacturing centres tended increasingly to specialise: Halifax, thanks respectively to the enterprise of its Akroyds and Crossleys, emerged pre-eminent in the production of damasks and fancy fabrics, and of carpets. 'Not many Kidderminster carpets are actually made at Kidderminster,' one proud Yorkshireman would boast, 'but enormous numbers of them are manufactured in Yorkshire, and the man who lays down a Brussels carpet in his house may feel pretty confident that it was made in Halifax.' Batley specialised in blankets, the Spen Valley in shoddy and mungo re-manufactured from 'the scraps and leavings and remnants of the other woollen and worsted industries'. In 1836 a Bradford manufacturer called Titus Salt began his experiments with alpaca wool from South America which would lead to the building of Saltaire.

The West Riding's iron and steel industry found a rival in the farthest North Riding following the exploitation of ironstone in the Cleveland Hills. In 1801 Middlesbrough had boasted a population of just 25 souls living in a few cottages on the flats at the mouth of the Tees: 50 years later it numbered 7,631, and by 1891 more than 75,000. Its growth was due, not only to its foundries—for which the opening up of ore at nearby Eston Nab in 1850 supplied the chief impetus—but to a combination of factors: it was linked early with the Stockton and Darlington Railway; town plans were drawn up by an enterprising body calling themselves the Owners of the Middlesbrough Estate; whilst its docks, operative from 1842, drew upon the developing iron production of all Tees-side. As one of the Owners, with remarkable vision, had confided to his diary in 1828: 'I was fancying the coming of a day when the bare fields we then were traversing would be covered with a busy multitude, and numerous vessels crowding to these banks denoting a busy seaport.'

Radical changes were affecting every walk of life, as age-old methods of national and local government proved inadequate in the face of industrialisation and growing population. The days of a system of Parliamentary representation that gave Members to small villages and none to flourishing towns, were clearly numbered, as were those of candidates' wining, dining and bribing of their privileged voters. In 1807, when three candidates— one of whom was the Hull-born slave trade abolitionist William Wilberforce—contested Yorkshire's two county seats, the poll lasted for 15 days whilst electors were conveyed, at their candidates' expense, to York to cast their votes. Coaches and gigs raced one another along the roads, packed with Whigs and Tories; toll-gates prudently stayed open. Wilberforce's supporters found novel means of rallying to him. 'No carriages are to be procured,' explained one of his agents, for they had started campaigning rather later than the opposition, 'but boats are proceeding up the river heavily laden with voters; farmers lend their waggons; even donkeys have the honour of carrying voters for Wilberforce, and hundreds are proceeding on foot.' Tempers reached inflammable heights: simply by shouting 'Milton for ever!' (one of the candidates) a boy precipitated a riot at Leeds. Wilberforce, who came top of the poll, ran up expenses of nearly £70,000; his opponents between them £200,000. One not untypical inn treated voters to the tune of £1,389 4s in wines alone.

The Reform Act of 1832 increased Yorkshire's Parliamentary representation from 30 to 37 Members, redistributing seats on a fairer basis. The 'rotten borough' of Hedon and the 'pocket boroughs' of Aldborough and Boroughbridge were disenfranchised (and the shining career of Michael Thomas Sadler incidentally and sadly scotched); two Members were allocated to each Riding instead of two to the entire county as heretofore. Northallerton and Thirsk, which had each enjoyed two Members, were reduced to one each; Whitby was given one. At last, if belatedly, West Riding manufacturing towns were represented: Leeds, Sheffield, Halifax and Bradford were each given two Members, Huddersfield and Wakefield one each. At the same time, the extension of the suffrage to householders paying £10 a year rent, benefited only the middle class and left the poorer still a voteless majority; not until 1868 and another redistribution of seats that further strengthened the industrial areas at the expense of the agricultural, would smaller householders be given the vote.

The Reform Act did not produce an overnight political Utopia, neither did it miraculously bring any sudden decorum to electioneering. That same year, Sadler was defeated at Leeds by the historian Macaulay and manufacturer John Marshall, who at one point found himself confronted with 'a standard representing a view of Messrs Marshall's mill, in Water Lane, in a snow storm on a winter's morning, with several poor, decrepid, and half-naked children trudging in a shivering attitude through the snow'; which 'obnoxious banner' became the centre of a struggle in which bludgeons and poles were wielded and many injured, four seriously. At Huddersfield the Riot Act was read and troops called in to quell 'outrageous proceedings'.

Working-class attempts to extend the suffrage to all adult males, and to broaden the range of Parliamentary candidates by paying Members and abolishing their property qualification, found an outlet in the Chartist movement. In 1839 a London Working Men's Association organised such a petition, signed by 1,200,000 people, which was literally rolled into the House of Commons in the form of 'a cylinder of parchment, about the diameter of a coach wheel'. Its rejection sparked off a series of provincial riots, and the more violent West Riding malcontents collected guns and pikes like the Luddites before them, harrangued by hungry orators. 'Provide yourselves with knives,' exhorted one of these, 'good long knives, and then when the beef comes you will be ready.' A wild pathetic scheme for a wholesale Yorkshire rising and a march on London was nipped in the bud at Bradford, where men had been drilling openly on Fairweather Green. Depressed trade and general hardship occasioned a further outbreak in 1842, when striking workers from Stalybridge in Lancashire started a wave of disaffection which spread into Yorkshire — their method of stopping work in mills disinclined to join them, by forcing in the plugs of their boilers and dowsing their fires, named their episode the Plug Riots. 'I well remember the savage appearance of a huge crowd of men as they marched through Horton to Bradford,' one eye-witness related. 'They came pouring down the wide road in thousands, taking up its whole breadth — a gaunt, famished-looking desperate multitude, armed with huge bludgeons, flails, pitch-forks and pikes, many without coats and hats, and hundreds upon hundreds with their clothes in rags and tatters'; he saw one wretch die after eating raw potatoes on a stomach empty for two days. Troops and police doubled out to meet them (the Leeds authorities had apprehensively ordered some 30,000 special constables' staves), but several days of rioting throughout the West Riding accomplished nothing save damaged property and broken heads, and a commission at York sentencing ringleaders to spells of imprisonment.

Other social measures, increasingly necessary for the developing communities of the century's opening decades, served to exacerbate ill-feeling and provoke hostility. The Poor Law Amendment Act of 1834 improved on a basically Elizabethan system of relief by transferring responsibility from parish vestrymen to locally-elected Guardians of the Poor answerable to a central Local Government Board. Haphazard outdoor relief was discouraged in favour of the more heavily-institutionalised charity of Union workhouses, wherein the separation of children from adults would seem, in the light of Eden's findings a generation earlier, by no means simply a callous gesture. Yet Anti-Poor Law orators emotionally christened the new workhouses 'Bastilles' and the Amendment Act a 'Catechism of Hell', whilst the hapless Commissioner appointed to implement its measures in the West Riding was assaulted in Bradford and his face beaten black and blue. One by one, however, the Yorkshire Boards of Guardians were perforce formed: one of the last was at Todmorden, whose MP John Fielden combined Anti-Poor Law principles with factory reform.

The Corn Laws provided another source of discontent. Those of 1815 had stipulated that no foreign corn might be imported duty-free until the home price reached 80s per quarter, thereby keeping prices high in favour of the landowners, against a background of recurring bread riots, rick-burnings and hardships propagandised by Ebenezer Elliott, Sheffield iron-merchant and Corn Law Rhymer:

> *Child, is thy father dead?*
> *Father is gone!*
> *Why did they tax his bread?*
> *God's will be done!*

Only after years of agitation and strenuous campaigning by an Anti-Corn Law League led by Richard Cobden and John Bright, voicing the instincts of the industrial masses, were the hateful Laws repealed in 1846. The West Riding received the news with a jubilation auguring an exaggerated estimate of forthcoming benefits, firing cannon and ringing church bells, one firm sticking a huge loaf atop their works labelled 'Free Traders of Holbeck'. In Leeds they held a fireworks display, an 'equestrian troupe' performed on Woodhouse Moor, and aeronaut Charles Green made a balloon ascent from the White Cloth Hall. 'When we got the repeal of the Corn Laws,' a Keighley man would remember, 'my father bought some beef and other things, and he ordered my mother to make a good dinner; and when we sat down to it my mother stood over the table and cried, and said: "I have lived a long while in this world and never before saw a meal like this, nor never heard tell of such".'

FURTHER READING

Chapter 7
Edward Baines: *History, Directory and Gazetteer, of the County of York*, 1822.
James Berry: *The Luddites in Yorkshire*, 1970.
James Burnley: *The History of Wool and Woolcombing*, 1889.
W. B. Crump, M.A., and Gertrude Ghorbal, M.A.: *History of the Huddersfield Woollen Industry*, 1935.
William Cudworth: *Worstedopolis: a Sketch History of the Town and Trade of Bradford, the Metropolis of the Worsted Industry*, 1888.
Ian Dewhirst: *Gleanings from Victorian Yorkshire*, 1972.
J. S. Fletcher: *The Making of Modern Yorkshire, 1750–1914*, 1918.
William Lillie: *The History of Middlesbrough*, 1968.
Frank Peel: *The Risings of the Luddites, Chartists and Plug-Drawers*, 1895.
E. Royston Pike: *Human Documents of the Industrial Revolution in Britain*, 1966.
Fred Singleton: *Industrial Revolution in Yorkshire*, 1970.
Charles Wing: *Evils of the Factory System, Demonstrated by Parliamentary Evidence*, 1837.

8
Victorian Yorkshire

The nineteenth century inaugurated an ease and speed of communication that shrank distances and offered a mobility which would have seemed unbelievable to any earlier generation. Georgian road and vehicle improvements had by 1768 cut down the journey from Leeds to London to two and a half days, and a decade later to 39 hours. Coaches were averaging speeds of eight miles an hour, faster than the postboys who carried the mails. The transference of the Royal Mail to stage coaches, completed in 1786, opened a glamorous 50-year era of dashing travel, with its accompaniment of guards' key-bugles and clattering inn-yards, so tellingly evoked by Dickens. The journey from Leeds to London was trimmed to 26 hours (1785), then to 21 (1815). York to London took only 20 hours; Hull and Leeds were five hours apart; York and Leeds but three.

The coaching age fostered a stirring vocabulary of inns and vehicles. From the Reindeer and the Ram at Doncaster, for example, ran in 1822 the *Rockingham* for London and the *Lord Nelson* for York, the *Defiance* for Sheffield, the *Rodney* for Hull, the *Royal Forester* for Nottingham and the *John Bull* to Thorne, 'whence passengers are immediately conveyed by Packet to Hull' . . . from the Black Boy went the *Highflyer* to London and the *Commander-in-Chief* for Sheffield and Birmingham . . . from the Old Angel, the post coach *Union* for London, from the New Angel the *Lord Wellington* to Huntingdon and Ware, and Royal Mails for London and Edinburgh, Newcastle and Glasgow. Stables and inns bustled with activity day and night; drivers were a breed apart. Dr Whitaker, probably unjustly, decried stage-coach travel because he opined passengers were at the mercy of 'a drunken brute'; and when four Methodist ministers complained of a dangerous journey to a Leeds proprietor, he cautioned his driver: 'Now, Tom, no racing on any account, mind you, or I'll discharge you—and I will discharge you, too, if you dare to let the "Pilot" beat you into Wakefield!' On the other hand, a coachman of the *Invincible* prided himself on his ability to pull up against inn-doors so that his passengers could alight straight on to the steps without soiling their boots on the muddy road. Another, a driver of the Doncaster *Highflyer*, also painted inn-signs and coach-doors and developed into the artist John Frederic Herring, famous for his pictures of horses.

Yet the realities of stage-coaching could be hard. It was an expensive means of travel: by the 1840s an inside seat cost as much as fourpence a mile, and an outside one, at the mercy of the elements, was only one-third cheaper. The letters of semi-literate travellers are anything but heartening. One woman saved up for eight months before undertaking a journey from the Lake District

58 The hazards of coaching: a spot of trouble on the York Flying Coach to London

into Yorkshire, being meanwhile in a state of constant apprehension as to her health and the weather; then she was 'verry powerly' for ten days after the return trip. When she wrote of her brother 'bean Afraid my intended Jurney to youre plase would inger my helth', she was, one feels, voicing a common sentiment.

But stage-coach travel, even whilst reaching fresh standards of speed and reliability, was doomed through competition in the slightly unlikely guise of the 'locomotive' steam engines. The railways did not come suddenly nor grandly, but piecemeal to begin with, against dire predictions of explosion and disaster. Yorkshire's first passenger line commenced between Leeds and Selby in 1834; its Marsh Lane Tunnel was the first in England to engulf an apprehensive train-load of citizenry—'the carriages,' noted one early awe-struck traveller, 'were open trucks with seats round.' The inaugural trip took two hours to cover the first 4½ miles, but the return journey managed to get from Selby to Leeds in an hour and a quarter. 1836 saw the introduction of a line between Pickering and Whitby, hopefully meant to infuse new life into the latter port, whose whaling, alum and ship-building industries were in decline. Its carriages were, for the first decade of its existence, horse-drawn and individually named *Lady Hilda*, *Premier* and *Transit*; its staff were known as postillion-riders; and it was in effect an extension of stage coaches running on rails. Nonetheless, it opened to a pealing of church bells, the strains of the Whitby Brass Band, and the lyric flights of versifiers:

Along the river's winding shore,
Or o'er its pebbly strand,
A road appears unknown of yore,
By modern science planned.

And as up Eskdale's ample range
It skirts each wood and dene,
More grand, more varied is each change,
More lovely grows the scene.

Thereafter the iron rails spread out across the landscape with ever-elaborating tentacles: Rotherham to Sheffield; Selby to Hull; Normanton to York, York to Darlington; Leeds to Bradford . . . For a time, stage coaches plied between stations plugging dwindling gaps in the railway network, only to be outclassed in the face of this new, fast, cheap mode of travel for the masses that was superseding both roads and canals.

The railway-building era wrote a flamboyant chapter into the annals of once-isolated places. Nothing better exemplifies this epic of the prodigal Victorian world than the Settle to Carlisle line, which brought a cosmopolitan, ever-changing army of navvies and masons, engineers and dynamiters swarming on to bleak inhospitable moors to accomplish not one but several wonders of their day. Blea Moor Tunnel was their tour de force: they started it in 1870 and finished in 1875; it cost £45 a yard, was 2,629 yards long and as much as 500 feet underground. Here, for years, 16 gangs laboured simultaneously—one from each end and two from each of seven shafts—in appalling weather, bad air and candle-light (the monthly bill for candles was £50). The sodden earth soaked up materials like a sponge. Intake Bank swallowed 12 months' tipping without visible effect; whilst Dandry Mire, having defied embankment builders for two years, was bridged by a viaduct instead. At Arten Gill navvies had to cut down over 50 feet into the moor before striking a firm rock base for their arches. For transporting equipment, vehicles called bog-carts were devised, rolled on barrels instead of wheels, but the

59 A typically 'stupendous work' of the railway-building era: the Crimple Valley viaduct, on the York and North Midland Railway

horses that pulled them often sank up to their middles. Lonely landscapes suddenly and temporarily became urban, with navvies' camps of wooden, felt-roofed huts in seas of mud, resembling, according to one visitor, 'the gold diggers' villages in the Colonies'. North of Ribblehead, at Batty Green or Batty Wife Hole, sprang up a rip-roaring shanty town housing more than 2,000, complete with a school, a library and a mission, a post office and a hospital. It was notable for bare-knuckle fights, and for herds of beef driven up on the hoof to satisfy the traditional appetites of navvies who lived, worked and played hard, and all too often died at their work. At Chapel-le-Dale lie buried 100 whom accident, smallpox and the climate brought to a premature end.

By the 1840s the proliferation of railway schemes and the floating of companies had reached the proportions of a mania— in 1845 were proposed no fewer than 76 lines affecting Yorkshire. At the centre of a gigantic web of speculation and corruption thrived, for awhile, the amazing George Hudson, 'the Railway King', erstwhile draper, promoter and chairman of the York Union Bank, thrice Lord Mayor of York, MP for Sunderland. 'He is about five feet eight inches in height,' wrote a contemporary, 'of a stout burly frame, with a short bull-neck, surmounted by a head not conspicuous for intellectuality.' Intellect or no, he virtually controlled the railways of the North and Midlands and made his fortune many times over; only to fall into bankruptcy and disgrace following the eventual collapse of his empire and investigation of his affairs. Indignant and fickle citizens of York renamed Hudson Street a still not inappropriate Railway Street, and dismantled a statue they had previously honoured him with, somewhat ungratefully forgetting that, thanks to his efforts, York remained an important railway centre, grafting a humming wagon-works, engineering, glass and chocolate industries upon its ancient glories.

Yet industrialisation and the centralising of populations served to exacerbate problems inherent for centuries, as towns and cities, too rapidly growing, outstripped the capacities of their sanitation and water supplies. Local government bodies which had formerly scraped by, appeared increasingly inadequate; an uneven miscellany of select vestries, churchwardens and manor courts faced situations beyond their control. Their half-trained surveyors and unpaid constables had become, by the nineteenth century, an anachronism; sanitary inspectors and medical officers of health were unheard-of. Meanwhile, the teeming, multiplying poor simply had not enough houses, no amenities, and nobody had formed any conception of the dangers of pollution.

West Riding towns especially presented a nauseating spectacle of dung-heaps and rotting garbage. 'A most filthy open drain or sump in yard,' related a wholly typical mid-century observer of the unseemlier corners of Keighley, 'eleven pigcotes and eleven swill-tubs about the premises, in a most disgraceful state. Large quantities of manure laid about, the whole sending forth the most odious stinks, that it is really astonishing how anybody can live in the neighbourhood. Two privies adjoining these premises in a state not fit for use, being so very dirty, and one of them being so badly ventilated that the stench was suffocating, and above it is a room.' At Keighley, again typical, was a case of one privy being shared by 29 houses; another of three privies to 69 houses; and another of six privies to 90 houses (and some houses had no access to privies at all). In Bradford, excrement ran along the back-

60   *Working-class housing spawned by the Industrial Revolution—Dufton's Yard, Leeds*

streets through open channels—'the flow is tardy and the whole soil is saturated with sewage water'—and the main sewers discharged into a canal basin where 'in hot weather bubbles of sulphurated hydrogen are continually rising to the surface, and so much is the atmosphere loaded with the gas, that watch-cases and other materials of silver become black in the pockets of the workmen employed near the canal', which was jocularly known as River Stink. At Leeds, rubbish was habitually thrown out into the yards, and privies 'open to view both in front and rear' were left unemptied for six months at a stretch. Sheffield parents hardly felt it worthwhile to wash their children before putting them to bed, because 'their bodies imbibe continual dust and grime'. Halifax dwellers in the damp and filthy Folds were continually depressed by 'the effluvium which assails them at every step'; whilst residents of Marsh, near Huddersfield, asserted that 'the last time there was a swamp in New Hey Road you might have buried a horse' (this was felt to be an exaggeration, but the statement that 'a horse might have left his hind leg in it' was not).

Vile conditions were not limited to the main towns. At Pateley Bridge, in picturesque Nidderdale, people were taking water from open courses that received the contents of pigsties and privies: one medical gentleman could account for their comparative health only through 'the merciful providence of God'. Poor woolcombers in Haworth—due to its Brontë family associations, possibly the most over-romanticised community in Yorkshire—were living and sleeping in their combing-shops where windows were never opened: one family of seven slept in two beds among the tools of their trade. Haworth's 2,500 population by mid-century were sharing 69 privies, and a cesspit at the top of the main street overflowed down an open channel. On washday Monday mornings, in dry spells, women would start queuing with their buckets at the Head Well by two o'clock; this water supply, also for drinking, turned 'green and putrid' in summer, when cattle refused to taste it.

Almost everywhere was the same tale of ignorance and neglect. A Rivers Commission of 1866 described the Aire as 'abused, obstructed and polluted to an extent scarcely conceivable by other than eye witnesses', and horrifically catalogued the dumping of 'hundreds of thousands of tons per annum of ashes, slag and cinders from steam boiler furnaces, ironworks, and domestic

fires, of broken pottery and worn-out utensils of metal, refuse brick
from brick-yards and old buildings, earth, stone, and clay from
quarries and excavations, road scrapings, and street sweepings';
whilst 'hundreds of carcasses of animals, dogs, cats, pigs, etc.'
were to be seen floating on its waters or putrifying on its banks.
Between the 1830s and the 1860s the beds of some of the Aire's
tributaries had risen by four or five feet on accumulated rubbish.
A machine-maker along the North Beck blandly admitted: 'Our
place is a very awkward place, and we have to lead the ashes to the
land if we cart them away, therefore it is a great convenience to us
to be able to put them into the beck'—thereby saving £50 a year in
carters' wages.

The poor who inhabited the narrow courts, the wretched
dwellings and cheap lodging-houses—one at Huddersfield took
20 lodgers in four beds, another had 19 lodgers and no beds, and
rogues and 'trampers' at Keighley dossed-down on cellar floors-
tended easily towards an existence in which drinking, whoring,
pilfering and fighting provided recurring themes. The semi-
literate diary of a West Riding watchman, who preceded the
formation of a regular police force, catches them to the life: '$\frac{1}{2}$ p 12
Clock on Sunday morning Samuel Smith comonley caled Mucky
Sam thrown Patrick Waterhouse over the Batlment at damside a
depth of 5 yards & cut & wounded im daingerously . . . 12 Clock
on Saturday night the Lanlord at wool pack inn and William

Holt striped stark naked in the street fiting and 100 persons round them . . . ½ p 11 Clock on Tusday night Cathrinah Sullivan strowling the streets with 15 men put in the Lock up. . . .' Stated the Governor of York Castle in 1854: 'Nineteen out of every twenty who come under my care, come directly or indirectly, through drinking'; 98 of the 119 prisoners brought for trial at the previous summer's assizes had, it was emotionally claimed, 'declared that this bait of the devil's had been greedily swallowed by them and was the cause of their misfortunes'.

Pre-eminent in an era which prided itself on its good works, the temperance societies wrestled variously—Scarborough's split into 'gentlemen's' and 'working-men's' factions—for the minds and bodies of the drinking poor, publishing character-building magazines, holding galas and Grand Festivals, marching to a hearty repertoire of songs, and throwing up such occasionally endearing personalities as Bradford-born Thomas Worsnop, a converted drunkard who tramped the Yorkshire roads with a carpet-bag full of tracts and called impromptu meetings by waving a red flag and sounding an old watchman's rattle. He was known miscellaneously as 'the Great Apostle of Total Abstinence in the North of England', 'the Teetotal Garibaldi', 'the Flag and Rattle Man' or 'the Navvy Parson'; and his admirers sang a slightly tongue-in-cheek ditty about him:

> *Worsnop, the navvy parson,*
> *In thee we truly glory,*
> *For when thy steam is up*
> *Thou tells a wondrous story.*

> *He makes us laugh, and in a turn*
> *Our tears begin to flow;*
> *Such power no other mortal has,*
> *At least, none that we know.*

Illness and disease were rife: deaths were common from measles and whooping cough, scarlet fever and typhus fever, diphtheria, influenza, consumption . . . a Keighley woman, buried in her forty-fourth year after bearing 30 children who all died in infancy, supplies some sort of gruesome record; yet in colourful Haworth of the Brontës the average age of death was 25·8 years. An influx

THE TREE OF MISERY & DEATH.
WITH SOME OF ITS ROOTS LAID BARE.

Designed by G.Peake.

62   *Victorian temperance propaganda: 'The Tree of Misery and Death', published in 1876*

of Irish, during the Potato Famine of the 1840s, came stricken with typhus fever: at York a philanthropic citizen overcame the locals' natural reluctance to house sufferers, by building them a wooden hospital in the field of a tenant who sold milk, since 'the coos would not take fever'. Epidemics ran riot. In 1832, cholera struck down hundreds at York, Sheffield and most seriously Leeds, where a surgeon drew a sensible conclusion that 'the dreadful disease was most prevalent in those parts of the town which were situate in the vicinage of the river or large water courses', the neighbouring populace signifying their disapproval of a Cholera Hospital set up in St Peter's Square by breaking its windows. (This otherwise distressing episode was, however, enlivened by the more ingratiating eccentricities of human nature: a miller near Pontefract, who had served aboard the *Royal Sovereign* at Trafalgar, made his own coffin with ropes instead of handles, and with 'three rows of port holes painted black' along each side and the name of his ship on each end—happily he did not need it for another 12 years.) In 1847 came a typhus fever epidemic: an account of its ravages in Leeds includes such graphic statements as '28 persons had the fever in seven houses, three of which were without beds'; and the following year cholera was back again. Some of the authorities' precautions, circulated and placarded, are revealing: people were advised to change their clothes from time to time, and—'if available'—to indulge in 'occasional warm bathing'. More than 2,000 died in Leeds alone.

The struggle towards better conditions was long, difficult and uneven. In some towns, such as Harrogate and Huddersfield and Keighley, local Acts of Parliament created well-intentioned but largely euphemistic bodies called Improvement Commissioners, vesting the more solid citizens (to qualify for office they had to be worth £1,000) with authority for 'paving, lighting, cleansing, watching, regulating, and otherwise improving' their towns. Whilst they usually contrived to shine in some item, in introducing gas-lighting or building waterworks, the magnitude of their tasks too often outweighed both their capabilities and the limitations of their rate-levied finances, their responsibilities ranging from essentials like lighting and paving, through the diversities of policing, to the minutiae of discouraging the populace from firing guns, letting off squibs and slaughtering animals in the streets, and instructing dog-owners to muzzle their pets during rabies scares. In 1835 the Municipal Corporations Act brought the old chartered boroughs like York and Ripon, Leeds and Hull, on to a revised footing better able to cope with contemporary problems, and succeeding decades saw the awarding of borough status to Yorkshire's developing centres: Bradford, Halifax and Wakefield in the 1840s, Middlesbrough in the 1850s, Batley, Dewsbury and Huddersfield in the 1860s. . . . The North, East and West Riding County Councils came into existence under the Local Government Act of 1888.

Yet ultimately, it was the cholera epidemics which underlined the glaring deficiencies in sanitation and water supply, and gave point to the campaigning of the Manchester-born reformer Edwin Chadwick. His Public Health Act of 1848 authorised—indeed, compelled—the setting up of Local Boards of Health in districts whose death-rate reached 23 per thousand, or one-tenth of whose rate-payers petitioned for sanitary measures. Thereafter, albeit gradually and uncertainly, the worst evils were overcome by locally-elected bodies, answerable to a central authority, employing medical officers of health and inspectors of nuisances, to whom townspeople could, and vociferously did, complain. 'Sir,' declared one irate West Riding citizen, 'as the children, my wife and some friends were going to the Tarn on Thursday, the *Stink* from Mr Walbank's dead horse boiling place was so *sickening* that they had to put their handkerchiefs over their mouths and noses and rush past till they got to the other side of the building. Surely it is time that this *nuisance* was done away with . . .' And eventually, though often slowly, 'done away with' it was!

But if the vast majority of the working classes were to see out the century in their narrow slums, Victorian pride dictated the adornment, on a lavish scale, of their rising city centres. Smoky Bradford, anxious to patronise the 'cultural needs of a business metropolis', opened its St George's Hall in 1853, an imposing building hedged with Corinthian pillars, containing a restaurant 'for the accommodation of mercantile men' and a concert hall to seat 3,140, lit by 1,750 gas jets. 'We are eleven feet wider than the hall at Birmingham, and about as much longer,' delightedly observed the Mayor. 'We are exactly the same width as Exeter Hall, London, with greater length, a loftier ceiling and a much better arrangement of the audience.' The Bradford Town Hall, completed 20 years later, was distinguished by a spire modelled

63 *An aerial view of late Victorian Bradford, from William Cudworth's* Worsted-opolis *of 1888*

on the Campanile of the Palazzo Vecchio in Florence: it was 217 feet 6 inches high and involved 5,000 tons of stone. This building, further, bristled with the statues of 35 kings and queens, which an admiring public was allowed to view at close quarters, for sixpence—proceeds going to the Infirmary, the Fever Hospital and the Eye and Ear Hospital—before they were hoisted into their lofty positions. Meanwhile, in 1858, the Queen had opened the magnificent Leeds Town Hall, with an estimated 200,000 crowding the streets for a glimpse of Her Majesty amid a furore of ceremonial which the papers called 'one of the brightest events in local history'. It formed a massive parallelogram 250 feet by 200 feet, surrounded by Corinthian columns and pilasters; out of its centre rose the great Victoria Hall, richly decorated within, and deliberately out-distancing in size most other provincial halls and some even in London. Five years under construction, much of its stone had been quarried at nearby Rawdon Hill, the clerk of works keeping such a stern eye on quality that on one occasion he 'took a hammer and destroyed a cornice stone in order to prevent it being used in the building'. After Leeds, anybody else's Town Hall must have seemed somewhat of an anti-climax, though Morley strove after a similar, if less huge, effect.

Occasionally, and in the cause of industrialisation, towns came fully-fledged, as it were, without any sordid growing pains. Edward Akroyd was experimenting with a little model village at Copley, near Halifax, during the 1840s; but Yorkshire's classic example in this field belongs to Sir Titus Salt, a Bradford manufacturer grown wealthy on Peruvian alpaca. In 1850, deciding to integrate the work of his several scattered mills into one great factory, he began his 'Palace of Industry' near Shipley, then a 'pretty rural spot' along the River Aire, convenient to road, railway and the Leeds and Liverpool Canal—he and his architect and engineer jointly conjured up the name Saltaire. His gigantic Italianate mill boasted what was thought to be the longest workroom in the world, and a chimney ('It shall be an additional ornament to the place,' declared Salt) in the style of an Italian bell-tower; he even, after the 1851 Exhibition, considered acquiring the Crystal Palace as a weaving-shed! Round his 'Model Mill' he built a model town for his workers: more than 800 houses with 'every convenience and a plot of garden', laid out on a grid plan; 45 almshouses complete with pensions for the old and

64　*Sir Titus Salt, manufacturer and philanthropist (1803–1876)*

65　*Saltaire, a model mill town in rural surroundings*

infirm; schools and baths and wash-houses, and a 14-acre park; a Wesleyan Chapel and a handsome Congregational Church (for he was a Nonconformist) to which was added his family mausoleum; a Club and Institute intended (for he was a teetotaller) 'to supply the advantages of a public-house, without its evils'—there were no taverns in the model town.

Saltaire represented a philanthropic extension of that thoroughness and sometimes vulgar scale which the lucky successful manufacturers tended to lavish on their residences, for the stately home of the Victorian period is typically that of the newly-rich flamboyantly anxious to appear cultured. At Oakworth House, Isaac Holden employed French workmen 'for years' building an amazing rockery and summer-house lined with 'startling' mirrors; his winter garden alone cost him £30,000. Woodleigh Hall, at Rawdon, an 'ornamented Elizabethan' mansion of 1869, ran architectural riot with pinnacles, pilasters, colonnades, porticos and a 60-foot tower. Into vastly larger-than-life 1870s Cliffe Castle at Keighley, Henry Isaac Butterfield crammed a magpie's treasure-hoard including vases looted from the Pekin Summer Palace in the China War, a Siberian malachite fireplace, Napoleon III's tea-caddy and a copy, 'of large dimensions', of some Landseer deer; his bedroom furniture had belonged to Rossini, and 'the bed now used by Mr Butterfield is the same as that on which that eminent composer passed away to his rest'.

On the custom provided by the leisured wealthy, inland spas and coastal watering-places developed far beyond their homely Georgian proportions. One visited palmy Harrogate for its 'company', and, it was said, 'not to be seen on Scarborough Spa in the season was to be out of fashion and of no account'. Up went the great expensive hotels, the seaside laid out with promenades and marine drives. No less than Sir Joseph Paxton, designer of the Crystal Palace, was called in to remodel Scarborough's Spa in 1860 on the site of a more modest edifice blown out to sea in a gale; there the Prince of Wales listened to the orchestra and watched the plays in a Spa Theatre glittering with illuminations. Victorian faith in what was called the water cure transformed Ilkley from a village of thatched cottages, where invalids could hire asses to carry them up for a simple cold bath on the edge of the moors, to a dignified town thriving, after the manner of Worcestershire's Great Malvern, on its solid hydropathic establishments. Field sports provided another social milieu, Yorkshire's rolling acres hunted by such select packs as the Bedale, the Middleton, the Holderness, the Hackness. The York and Ainsty, on 4 February 1869 (on which date its 'large and brilliant field' was frozen, as it were, for posterity by the fortuitous publicity attending the upsetting of a ferryboat full of riders at Newby Hall), reads like an excerpt from Burke's Landed Gentry: Viscount Downe of Danby Lodge . . . Lord Lascelles of Harewood . . . Sir George Wombwell of Newburgh Park . . . Henry Frederick Clare Vyner of Newby Hall . . . William Ingilby of Ripley Castle . . . Sir Charles Slingsby of Scriven Park . . . One huntsman, drowned on the occasion, had been 'ardently devoted to the pleasures of the chase, and kept up a stud of fourteen horses, hunting six days a week'.

To move from the opulence of the rich to the poverty of the working classes points a contrast perhaps a trifle glib; yet a yawning gulf indeed separated the new mansions from both the town slums of factory hands and the damp cottages of agricultural labourers. 'The weavers in Cononley were so poor,' one Victorian succinctly reminisced, 'they could only afford meat at Christmas and the Feast.' When, in the 1850s, a survey was made of the diet of some of the West Riding's hand woolcombers, then reduced by the decay of their trade to a pauperized class, their families were found to be 'rarely tasting animal food from year to year': an occasional sheep's head comprised an event, and many simply never ate meat, 'unless ordered by the Union surgeon in case of sickness'. Repeatedly, the more coherent nineteenth-century poor stress a staple diet of porridge and potatoes, 'with a little fat now and again. We often had porridge three or four times a day. If we could only get a little old milk and treacle with it we used to consider we had quite a treat. But mostly we had to take it without. This oatmeal porridge was about the only food poor people could afford, besides potatoes, and in order to get even that they had to work very hard'. There can be few more pathetic stories than that of the old woman dying and asking for a last treat, who could imagine nothing finer than 'a toathree porridge with a little bit of butter in the middle'. One Union doctor graphically described his working population as suffering from 'mental and physical depression, bloodless features, obstinate diarrhoea, and a sense of either sinking or falling away'.

Not the least depressing aspect of the Victorian poor is the frequency with which they bore the brunt of death and deprivation in an era which, by virtue of its industrial and social changes, was prone to disasters; small nameless people in numbers and dozens and hundreds supply the varying statistics of recurring mill fires, mining accidents, boiler explosions—one at a Bingley bobbin mill in 1869 flung bits of machinery a quarter of a mile and hurled stones and scalding water into a playground teeming with children, eight of whom were killed on the spot. On 28 December 1882, a Bradford chimney, 85 yards tall, collapsed on to Newland Mills and killed 54 workers (the toll would have been much higher had not many of the hands gone home for their breakfasts at the time). Most of the dead were women and children: the date, as local lore would be quick to point out, was appropriately Innocents' Day. Disaster of a different kind struck Holmfirth in 1852, when the Bilberry Reservoir burst to send an estimated 86,248,000 gallons pouring down the Holme Valley, 'sweeping all before them,' relates a vivid account, 'throwing a four story mill down like a thing of nought, tossing steam engine boilers about like feathers, and carrying death and destruction in their progress': 77, 'so far as could be ascertained', lost their lives; though at least one versifier (a kind of Yorkshire McGonagall) refused to commit himself further:

How many houses was Destroy'd
and mills swept quite away
and many hands Left unimployd
the number I canot now say.

Yet the lot of the nineteenth-century working class included a number of redeeming features, not least in the realm of education. The Industrial Revolution had created a new type of workman, the mechanic, whose instruction, his more idealistic social superiors opined, would 'greatly tend to improve the skill and practice of those classes of men, who are so essentially conducive to the prosperity' of rising manufacturing towns. In 1800 Dr George Birkbeck, a Settle Quaker appointed professor of chemistry and natural philosophy at the Andersonian Institution in Glasgow, had noticed the 'intelligent curiosity' shown by operatives in the workshops making his scientific apparatus, and was moved to ponder: 'Why are these minds left without the means of obtaining that knowledge which they so ardently desire; and why are the avenues to science barred against them because they are poor?' When he introduced free lectures for workmen, his audience swelled from 75 to 500 in four nights.

It was to be another quarter-century before Birkbeck's adult educational experiment bore fruit in the Mechanics' Institute movement. Yorkshire's first was established at Leeds in 1824, in 'a confined and remote locality, at the back of Park-row'; its founders included industrialists John Marshall and Benjamin Gott, and Edward Baines of the *Leeds Mercury*, its sensible aim being 'to supply, at a cheap rate, the advantages of instruction in the various branches of science, which are of practical application' in trades and occupations. Leeds's example was rapidly followed throughout the county, from Halifax, Wakefield and Skipton to Hull and Scarborough, where Mechanics' Institutes sprang up largely promoted and financed by manufacturers, clergy and professional men, offering classes and lectures delivered both by paid instructors and local enthusiasts, predominantly in the sciences: a typical curriculum for 1828 included electricity, the mechanical powers, zoology, the steam engine, the properties of bodies, and respiration. Scientific apparatus was made available; libraries formed, from which in some cases fiction was excluded, purer exponents tending to regard the reading of novels as 'only another kind of mischievous excitement'. Wrote an early attender of a West Riding Institute: 'The members met during two evenings of the week, from eight to ten o'clock. The first hour of the four was spent in collecting the weekly contributions'— twopence per person—'the remaining three were occupied by the renewal of books, conversations, essays, or readings from such periodicals as the "Mechanics' Magazine" and others of a more literary character; occasional lectures were also given by the members, as well as by professional lecturers.' In the event, the Mechanics' Institutes failed to fulfil the loftier hopes of their originators; as their novelty waned, popular appeal replaced solid instruction, and by the 1830s a peripatetic New Zealand chief and one Mrs Crowther, who performed on musical glasses, were proving their surest audience-catchers. This phase passed in turn: by the second half of the century, Institutes accommodated in more substantial premises were catering for a social and cultural spate of concerts, balls, oratorios, conversaziones and Saturday-night entertainments. At the same time, Yorkshire villages were exhibiting 'the same growing thirst for intellectual improvement which has long distinguished its manufacturing towns above other counties in Britain'. Mechanics' Institute libraries and news-rooms filled a need long before the adoption of the Public Libraries Act; as their classes offered unique opportunities to that large slice of society to whom regular education was still denied.

The means for both elementary and secondary instruction existed, though Lord Macaulay, speaking in Parliament, could paint an over-dramatic but perhaps not necessarily untypical picture of 'a room crusted with filth, without light, without air, with a heap of fuel in one corner and a brood of chickens in another; the only machinery of instruction a dog-eared spelling-book and a broken slate'. By the beginning of the century, many of the earlier endowed free and grammar schools had deteriorated through neglect and inadequate funds, their masters incompetent and their pupils dwindled, lucky if they could acquire an outmoded Greek and Latin and a grounding in 'reading, writing, and accounts'. For children whose parents could afford the fee, high-sounding private 'academies' proliferated: a Leeds directory of 1822 listed more than 50, whilst Sheffield boasted more than 60. These ranged from the good to the execrable, offering such practical subjects as commerce, French and geography, as well as tutoring young ladies in the gentler arts of drawing and needlework. Some Sunday Schools, bravely endeavouring to instil the rudiments, tackled a fairly hopeless task—repeatedly, witnesses to the Sadler Committee had described how they were tired out at the weekend, and fell asleep in Sunday School. Said one villager, of a school built by public subscription at Stanbury in 1805: 'Facing the scholars, the master had what we call a spindle chair, and in front of him was a three-legged table. On this table at times there were a dozen sticks that he had got out of the woods, and when any scholar was inattentive he would throw one of these sticks, and scarcely ever did he miss the child aimed at. During prayers more sticks went than at any other time'!

In 1805 a British and Foreign Schools Society, Nonconformist in origin, began opening its undenominational British Schools, thereby encouraging an alarmed Church of England to found a

National Society for Promoting the Education of the Poor in the Principles of the Established Church, and to lay out country-wide, between 1811 and 1870, an impressive £15,000,000 on what were conveniently termed National Schools. Other denominations, most notably the Roman Catholics and the Wesleyan Methodists, likewise opened schools which, state-aided to teach factory half-timers after 1833, coped barely, if at all in the towns, with large numbers of pupils. 'I have heard,' wrote a Yorkshire educationalist of the 1860s, 'of classes taught in the outer porch of the school because of the great crowd within, and I have seen a class assembled in the playground in order to escape the vitiated air and the Babel-like noise which I could hear going on inside'. Surviving log-books are eloquent both of over-strained masters and their difficulties in persuading regular attendances ('In the evening from 4 to 5 with pupil-teachers,' noted one eager new arrival at Oakworth, 'visited houses on Chip Hill to see if any new scholars could be got'), and of the lack or inadequacy of classrooms, desks, books and daily miscellanea—'very much tormented,' wrote one country teacher at his wits' end, 'with mice running across the floor, notwithstanding the noise.'

Ultimately, in 1870, it was a Bradford MP, William Edward Forster who, against the opposition of both Anglicans and Nonconformists, pushed through the Elementary Education Act which authorised the setting up of undenominational School Boards in educationally inferior districts. Ten years later, compulsory education was introduced, and in 1891 school fees were abolished. To be sure, there were no overnight miracles, and School Board elections tended to inject a new vituperation into the local politics of a generally robust era (the flinging of dead rats at public speakers was one of the less endearing gambits of the earthier type of Yorkshire electioneering); yet the marks and crosses of the illiterate, so common a feature in the documents of mid-century, were less pronounced by its close.

Gradually, too, workers were finding a voice through their trade unions. These had been forbidden between 1799 and 1824 by the Combination Acts, but had persisted nevertheless in the guise of sick clubs, whose paying out of funeral and sickness benefits could be extended to meet wider needs. A network of Combers' Clubs throughout Yorkshire and Lancashire provided hospitality for their members when 'tramping for work': each time an unemployed comber called without success at a combshop in search of a job, 'each clubman was required by the rules of the club to pay the man out of work one halfpenny', a practice not unnaturally resented by employers in times of industrial unrest. The Combination Acts notwithstanding, strikes flickered across the West Riding: Dewsbury mills were out, one after another, continuously from 1821 to 1823, and there were strikes at Wakefield in 1822 and again in 1824, when the repeal of the Acts brought trade unions out into the open. Bitterest of a crop of strikes occurred in 1825 at Bradford—so recently the scene of convivial Bishop Blaize festivities—when 20,000 woolcombers and stuff weavers came out in a 23-week battle against the manufacturers, their demands for an extra two to three shillings a week doomed to failure in the face of the deteriorating state of trade. At Scarborough and Whitby, the same year, the Seamen's Union prevented shipowners from recruiting non-union crews, intimidation rearing its ugly head when six blackleg sailors were 'dragged from their inn by a mob and forced to return home' to Bridlington. Occasionally, the worst violence flared: during a cloth-workers' strike at Farsley in 1832, a non-striking young Irishman was assaulted by 30 to 40 men and fatally injured. 'Although a large reward was offered for the apprehension of the murderers,' it was succinctly reported, 'they escaped.' It transpired also at the inquest that local union members had sworn a melodramatic oath whereby, if violated, 'their souls may be burnt in the lowest pit of Hell to all eternity'.

Employers replied by forming their own associations to combat the more 'unjust and pernicious' trade unions, by dismissing union workers and sympathisers (during the Bradford strike they sacked children whose parents were members of the Union Association of Woolcombers and Stuff Weavers), and by declaring general lock-outs in areas where selected mills had been brought out on strike. When the Saddleworth Weavers' Union struck in the winter of 1828, a retaliatory Master Clothiers' Society threatened legal action against landlords allowing their inns to be used for union meetings: the result, predictably, was the defeat of the weavers' union. But though most of the struggles of early, localised unions ended in failure, their officials were gaining invaluable experience, and the 1830s witnessed the emergence of broader-based if short-lived unions. The National Association for the

Protection of Labour, inspired by the Lancashire cotton spinners, attracted a number of Yorkshire subscriptions and survived for two years; John Tester, who had organised the Bradford combers' strike, tried heroically to weld the entire West Riding into one union; and in 1834 an abortive Grand National Consolidated Trades Union was vigorously supported by West Riding workers, who held mammoth protest meetings against their masters' insistence that they sign a bond renouncing all connection with it—though most of them would have to sign, eventually. Working-class disappointment over the 1832 Reform Act helped channel their energies into the Chartist movement, and not until the latter half of the century did trade unions re-emerge in a better organised and more palpable form. The Miners' Association employed a full-time solicitor; the Amalgamated Society of Engineers thrashed out a structure of head office, branches and general secretary; whilst a Sheffield Association of Organised Trades, established in 1859, called a national meeting of union delegates seven years later which pointed the way towards the first Trades Union Congress. It was at Sheffield too that an over-excited Grinders' Union, during an 1866 lock-out, resorted to the use of explosives, so alienating public opinion that union leaders, fearful of repressive repercussions, were encouraged to sink their differences of opinion into a moderate but ultimately more effective front.

At the same time, working-class enterprise was combating high prices, employers' 'tommy' shops that swallowed workers' wages, and a widespread adulteration of foodstuffs—flour mixed with alum and china clay, short-weight butter, currants and raisins rubbed in treacle to make them heavier—with the Co-operative movement. As early as 1797, some 'poor inhabitants' of Hull, distressed by the 'exorbitant price of flour', had clubbed together to build their own mill, a venture that proved so successful that the millers of the neighbourhood indicted it as a nuisance. A York jury 'considered poverty a still greater nuisance' and found in its favour, whereupon a second Hull Subscription Mill and a Whitby Union Mill followed suit. But the movement gathering momentum in the 1820s was largely inspired by the socialist ideals of economist-reformer Robert Owen, though most of the co-operative societies springing into being round Halifax and Huddersfield, and sometimes attempting over-ambitious manufacturing schemes in addition to trading, were doomed to the same bold failure as that visionary's Utopian colonies. Yet a seed had been sown, to reappear towards mid-century in the more realistic shape originated by the 28 Rochdale Equitable Pioneers of 1844, a medley of Owenites, self-styled social reformers and disappointed Chartists, who opened their humble store on a capital of £28, dividing their profits in proportion to their purchases. Steadily, thanks to this magic formula of 'dividend on purchase', colloquially the 'divi' (strategically paid out twice a year, for holidays and Christmas), a new and more stable wave of retail co-operatives grew up across the manufacturing districts of Lancashire and Yorkshire alike. 'We're going to have a "Co-op" Shop of our own,' one founder-member's cry to his skimping young wife voiced the general enthusiasm, 'we're doing business for such as ye.' Stores opened in cramped cottages and back-street warehouses; early members took turns minding the shop; at Keighley the treasurer smuggled the takings home every night and hid them in a linen-chest, whilst a crisis occasioned by over-stocking with ham was astutely weathered by holding a public tea; the Halifax society contrived to lost £81, whereupon irate members stormed the committee-room. Setbacks notwithstanding, by 1875 there were more than 130 co-operative societies in Yorkshire, 120 of these in the West Riding, developing in many directions: Leeds ran a corn-mill, made boots, undertook tailoring and building; Keighley wove wire mattresses and manufactured mangles; Greenfield let its own houses at low rents to members; co-operatives set up libraries and news-rooms, conducted funerals, became a comprehensive facet in the lives of the later Victorian poor. . . .

The nineteenth century enjoyed, moreover, a striking increase in the number and variety of denominational places of worship, Nonconformism putting down fertile roots alike in the mill towns and the broad country acres of Yorkshire. The New Jerusalem or Swedenborgian doctrine found early supporters in the West Riding; and Spiritualism, crossing the Atlantic a generation or so later, gained its first English mouthpiece in the *Yorkshire Spiritual Telegraph* which commenced publication in Keighley Market in 1855. Repeatedly, industrialists and employers fostered the chapel-going habit in their work-people. 'We wish and expect,' declared Jonas Sugden and Brothers, staunch

Methodists of Vale Mill at Oakworth, 'that every person in our employ attend some place of Divine Worship every Lord's Day'; likewise, 'that every youth, dependent upon those whom we employ, attend some Sunday and Day School, from the age of six years and upwards'.

The whole of the eighteenth century had produced 39 Independent or Congregational churches throughout the county; now, between 1800 and 1830, came another 63; from 1830 to 1870, a further 76; from 1870 to 1900, 56, ranging from fashionable town and city erections to tiny rural chapels, yet all imbued with a hardy determination. That at Settle, not untypical of mid-century Dales chapels, carried a debt for decades; its floors boasted no matting, its pulpit stairs no carpet; heated by means of an iron stove, its atmosphere was alternately smoke-filled or damply musty, its gallery virtually unusable in winter; for years a solitary bass fiddle provided its occasional sole musical accompaniment—otherwise, tunes were simply 'pitched'. One remote chapel, hard against the Lancashire border at Martin Top, which could not 'be described even as a hamlet, as there is only one house and shop anywhere near it', contrived to engage 'some of the best lay preachers in Yorkshire'.

Religious and social life were inseparable, church and chapel finances demanding a succession of fêtes, concerts, At Homes, exhibitions, their calendars highlighted by festivals, knife-and-fork teas, Sunday School anniversaries and open-air 'charities'. Victorian Whit Mondays thrilled to annual 'Walks' or, as one newspaper expressed it, 'the leading forth of the Sunday scholars from all parts of the town to the green fields in long procession'. Chapel minute-books record months of preparation: 'Resolved that the children have each a Cake & Beer given them, same as last year on Monday afternoon next. That they meet in the School Room at half past 1 o'clock P.M. & that Mr Saunders be requested to give an address, & afterwards they walk in the best order which can be arranged from the Chapel past Bridge-House, on the new Lees Road & return by Mill Hey to School, where they are to have Cake & Beer given them' (as the era progressed, the beer was replaced by 'lemon ale'). Women baked mountains of plain loaves and spice loaves for the occasion, cakes and plain crackneys and currant crackneys; bands perfected their hymn tunes.

The developing social activities of the Victorian age brought all walks together, as never before, in however self-conscious a mingling. Agricultural shows, springing into being, divided their exhibitors nicely into Gentlemen's, Farmers' and Labouring Men's classes; pig-breeding became a popular hobby among West Riding weavers, at a halcyon time when '$\frac{1}{4}$ lb. of Irish moss and 3 lbs. of Indian meal', boiled in 16 gallons of water, would make enough 'very strong jelly' to keep a large pig for a week, at a cost of sixpence! Workaday men fired by the glamour of uniforms enrolled in volunteer rifle companies, paying from five guineas to 12s a year according to rank, and subject to fines for such unhappy misdemeanours as 'careless use of the Sword or Sword Bayonet, or for wounding with it any other Member of the Corps'. Opportunities for sport presented themselves, through the formation of cricket and football and angling clubs. Political clubs catered for all shades of opinion against a background clicking of billiard balls. Brass bands, orchestral bands, reed bands, concertina bands, concert parties enjoyed a never-ending round of engagements. . . .

All the while, local authorities growing in stature and confidence, and backed by generous individuals, were increasingly providing public amenities like museums and libraries and parks, the latter especially a feature of the period. Named after their donors or the topical figures of their day—Beaumont Park at Huddersfield, Norfolk Park at Sheffield, Peel Park at Bradford, Albert Park at Middlesbrough—they offered cramped street-dwellers a space both for genteel promenading and for livelier recreation; for the century's progress included a subtle tempering of holiday entertainments. In its earlier and middle decades, the twice-yearly horse and cattle fairs had furnished highlights in the round of each community in turn (Barnsley and Dewsbury in May, Bawtry at Whitsuntide, Wakefield and Wetherby in November), main thoroughfares given up for several days on end to a bawling, jostling maelstrom of livestock and dealers, farm labourers standing for hire, mill-hands on holiday, locals away in service come briefly home, and all the fickle fun of the fair (at Bradford's, in 1823, 18 pickpockets were caught). Colourful albeit down-at-heel showmen thronged the travelling roads, with dancing bears, performing dogs, dioramas, trained fish; quacks and actors vied with menageries and circuses. One Sam Wild, proprietor of a Halifax-based company of Strolling Players, bought two camels captured in the Crimean War, and for a

66   The emergence of the seaside holiday: goat-cart on Scarborough sands

couple of years thereafter extracted impressive amounts of coppers
from the pockets of gaping Yorkists and Lancastrians—the bones
of Sultana, the female camel dying on tour at Skipton, were
packed off in hampers to the museum of the Halifax Literary and
Philosophical Society. On a more spectacular scale, the British
and Continental Equestrian Establishment, itinerating through the
West Riding in 1853, boasted a marquee accommodating 2,000
spectators and featured a 'wild' horse 'that was caught in the
wilderness of the Comanches, America'; nevertheless, its audiences
preferred the old, tried favourites, like the Equestrian Drama,
'Dick Turpin's Ride to York'.

But during the latter half of the century, as multiplying traffic
and tramlines pushed the old fairs out of main streets, temperance
and friendly societies and a variety of worthy causes realised the
fund-raising potential of mass entertainment by organising galas.
For a few days each year, parks resounded to brass bands,
merry-go-rounds, fireworks displays and homely performers with
bizarre names: Jap Van Laren and his quaint comic slack wire

act, Professor Rennef, the King of the Cannon Ball, the Marvellous Dunlops, the Zamezou Troupe of Lightning Acrobats. . . . For 80 years Bradford hosted a Great West Riding Gala in Peel Park, and a Keighley Cottage Hospital drew a comfortable portion of its early finances from revels laid on by local friendly societies in Victoria Park. Here it was, in 1898, that a trial of the then popular balloon ascent and parachute descent went spectacularly amiss, leaving a Captain Frederick Bidmead, his parachute entangled in the netting of his balloon, to dangle precariously through the clouds for 27 miles, coming painfully to earth near Pontefract. 'You are not likely,' he coolly described his experience to a reporter, 'to let go your grip when you know your life is dependent upon it'; and the newspaper-reading public loved him.

For with the spread of elementary education, and the abolition of the stamp duties which had bedevilled pre-Victorian newspapers, the working classes became avid regular readers. The *Leeds Mercury*, under the editorship of father and son Edward Baines, emerged as a penny daily voicing the Liberal sentiments of its period, anti-Corn Laws, anti-Poor Law Amendment Act and generally anti-factory reform. Its eighteenth-century Tory rival, the *Leeds Intelligencer*, never enjoyed quite the same extensive circulation, and in 1866 was absorbed by the mighty *Yorkshire Post*, which, in 1934, was also to swallow the *Mercury*. Other influential city papers included the *Bradford Observer*—later the *Yorkshire Observer*—the *Sheffield Times* and the *Sheffield Daily Telegraph*; whilst smaller journals proliferated in towns and rural parishes, although, as that prolific turn-of-the-century spectator of the Yorkshire scene, J. S. Fletcher, would observe: 'Smart young men who wish to educate the rural communities through their "Gazettes" or "Advertisers", and who publish leading articles of the college essay sort, and paragraphs which are meant to be clever and are only cryptic, soon discover that the news of a calf with two tails, or of a potato weighing five pounds, is vastly preferred.'

This generalisation could be applied to the wider field of literature. To be sure, the three Brontë sisters, writing from the imagination-catching setting of their moorside Parsonage at Haworth, would become the county's overwhelmingly most renowned authors of this—or of any other—era; yet Yorkshire household reading was nurtured on the highly recitable and fiercely regional contents of flimsy yearly publications such as *The Bairnsla Foak's Annual, an' Pogmoor Olmenack, The Halifax Original Illuminated Clock Almanac,* and *The Nidderdill Olminac.* A vigorous tradition of anonymous dialect versifying, earthily descriptive of the life of dales and fells and coastline, drew its inspiration from such unpoetic material as, typically, a dead pig:

> *T'owd pig's got mezzles* [measles] *an' she's deead, poor thing.*
> *An' what will you mak o' her poor awd heead?*
> *'T will mak as good a yune* [oven] *as iver baked breead.*
> *An' what will you mak o' her poor awd legs?*
> *As good a set o' bed-props as iver propped beds.*
> *An' what will you mak o' her poor awd skin?*
> *'T will mak as good a blanket as iver man lay in.*
> *An' what will you mak o' her poor awd tail?*
> *'T will mak as good a hammer-shaft as iver drove a nail.*
> *An' what will you mak of her poor awd lugs?* [ears]
> *As good a pair o' bed-flops as iver flopped bugs.*

The nineteenth century nurtured a scribbling host of variously-inspired factory workers, schoolteachers, grocers, lead-miners, druggists, engine-drivers, farmers and warpdressers, drawing realistic subject-matter and simple philosophy from their everyday surroundings. If they swung too readily towards extremes of comedy and pathos, and in the Victorian fashion waxed often sentimental, they nevertheless achieved a rich folk-literature, emphatic, in the West Riding at least, of hard conditions, poverty, malnutrition and premature death, surprisingly leavened with good-humour. Nobody better exemplifies the genre than Benjamin Preston, a Bradford woolsorter who raised himself to the status of a minor literary lion:

> *Ah'm a weyver, ye knaw, an' awf deead,*
> *So ah due all 'at ivver ah can*
> *To put away aht o' my eead*
> *The thowts an' the aims of a man.*
> *Eight shillin' i' t'wick's what ah arn*
> *When ah've varry gooid wark an' full time,*
> *An' ah think it's a sorry consarn*
> *For a fellah 'at's just in his prime.*

168

Bud ahr maister says things is as well
As they have been or ivver can be,
An' ah happen sud think so mysel'
If he'd nobbud swop places wi' me . . .

That last cocky pleasantry puts a difficult industrial relationship
into a human perspective.

FURTHER READING

Chapter 8
Tom Bradley: *The Old Coaching Days in Yorkshire*, 1889.
Asa Briggs: *Victorian Cities*, 1963.
Roy Brook: *The Story of Huddersfield*, 1968.
James Burnley: *Sir Titus Salt, and George Moore*, 1885.
Bradford Illustrated Weekly Telegraph: 'A Series of Picturesque Views
of Castles and Country Houses in Yorkshire', 1885.
R. and E. Frow and Michael Katanka: *Strikes: a Documentary
History*, 1971.
Horace Hird: *Bradford in History*, 1968.
Frederick W. Houghton and W. Hubert Foster: *The Story of the
Settle-Carlisle Line*, 1948.
Bernard Jennings, M.A., editor: *A History of Nidderdale*, 1967.
F. W. Moorman: *Yorkshire Dialect Poems (1673–1915) and Tradi-
tional Poems*, 1919.
A. J. Peacock and David Joy: *George Hudson of York*, 1971.
Beatrice Potter: *The Co-operative Movement in Great Britain*, 1910.
G. W. J. Potter: *A History of the Whitby and Pickering Railway*, 1906.
Percy Redfern: *The Story of the C.W.S.: The Jubilee History of the
Co-operative Wholesale Society Limited, 1863–1913*, 1913.
Rivers Commission: *Third Report of the Commissioners Appointed to
Inquire Into the Best Means of Preventing the Pollution of Rivers
(Rivers Aire and Calder)*, 1867.
Mabel Tylecote: *The Mechanics' Institutes of Lancashire and York-
shire Before 1851*, 1957.
Thomas Whitehead: *History of the Dales Congregational Churches*,
1930.

9
The Twentieth Century

The new century, at its beginning, presented a face still turned, in some respects, back towards the leisurely past rather than forward to a drastic future. 'The keeping or not keeping of domestic servants' could still be regarded as 'marking the division between the working classes and those of a higher social scale'. People still, in unchanging valleys and backward streets, compiled spells and witch charms, filled bottles with hair and urine and hid them under floorboards, buried mummified sheeps' hearts stuck with pins to ward off ailments, and transmuted a high incidence of tapeworms into a superstitious mythology of water-wolves, little animals which moved about inside your stomach, lived on the food you ate, and slept each night with their heads on your heart. Communities still made of their exhibitionists and mental defectives a sometimes laughable, sometimes pathetic folklore, wherein workaday figures attained racy nicknames: Old Fletch, Diddum Smith, Ned Pompom, Flywheel Tommy, Bull Jack, Johnny Pot Taw. . . .

Pent-up emotions found an outlet in the demonstrative, ingenuous patriotism that named streets and parks and hospitals after Queen Victoria and her Jubilees; that massed schoolchildren with pewter medallions in their coats to line flag-bedecked roads and cheer town and village Coronation festivities; that gave enthusiastic send-offs to Reservists, Volunteers and Yorkshire Hussars marching off for the South African War: 'I only hope,' jingoistic dignitaries were able to encourage their local soldiers in 1900, 'that if you have a chance you will make it a hot corner for a few Boers somewhere.' The Czarist Navy's panicky shelling of Hull trawlers on the Dogger Bank in 1904 (they mistook them for

67 *Turn-of-the-century patriotism: men of the 3rd Volunteer Battalion Duke of Wellington's (West Riding) Regiment prior to departure for the Boer War*

Japanese torpedo-boats) occasioned vociferous, though happily unheeded, public demands for a war with Russia.

In practical terms, the lot of the poorer classes remained little alleviated by Victorian advances, though perhaps their own nature could in part be blamed for that. In 1901 Benjamin Seebohm Rowntree, the sociologist-director of a progressive York cocoa and confectionery firm, published his *Poverty: a Study of Town Life*, the results of a painstaking investigation into the circumstances of 11,560 York families, and put his finger unerringly upon 'the chief characteristics of slum life—the reckless expenditure of money as soon as obtained, with the aggravated want at other times; the rowdy Saturday night, the Monday morning pilgrimage to the pawnshop, and especially that love for the district, and disinclination to move to better surroundings, which, combined with an indifference to the higher aims of life, are the despair of so many social workers'. He found no fewer than 20,302 people, or 27·84 per cent of the city's population, living in poverty, more than a third of them verging on destitution. His investigators' notebooks catalogued the sorry details of ill-health and malnutrition, dirt and wretchedness, of numerous families sharing common closets and water-taps. Poor housewives of the more industrious sort, asked how they budgetted for occasional essentials such as new boots, repeatedly replied, 'We have to get it out of the food money and go short'. Yet one young man, who had married a 'superior' girl and graduated into a 'respectable' street, voiced an attitude that was not uncommon: 'At home,' he said, 'we had meals when we liked—the kettle was on the hob, and some food on the table. But now I have to sit down properly—there's always a tablecloth on the table, that I mustn't mess up, and altogether things aren't half so comfortable!'

The agricultural poor fared no better. 'How to stop the steady drift of the population to the towns?' questioned the opening sentence of Rowntree's study of rural labour problems in 1913 — the rural population of England and Wales had declined from 49·8 per cent of the whole in 1851, to 21·9 per cent by 1911. Wages fluctuated with the weather and the crops. One North Riding family, its chief breadwinner a 'road-scraper' for eight months of the year and a farm worker around harvest-times, confessed that they would have found it 'almost impossible to live if the children who are out in service did not help those at home'. Another jobbing labourer of precarious income scraped by on selling garden produce and shooting rabbits, but sometimes 'all the rabbits have made off into a neighbour's land, or have taken the scare altogether'. A 'beast-man' with four children, living in a thatched cottage typically 'more picturesque than healthy', accounted a visit to a cattle show as his only luxury during an entire year: 'It isn't what you would call a living,' observed his wife, 'only a sort of putting on.' An East Riding woman was reduced to begging turnips off nearby farmers; though her husband, helping out at the village joiner's, had discovered an ironically profitable line making coffins, 'picking up' firewood as a perquisite.

In politics, at least, the working man was being championed by a pugnacious young Independent Labour Party game to take on both its established opponents. 'The difference between Liberal and Tory,' trumpeted its news-sheets, 'is pretty much that between upper and nether millstone. The quality of the two is essentially the same. They are sections of the wealth-possessing class, and on all questions affecting the Interest of Labour, they play into one another's hands.' The ILP's inaugural conference had been held at the Bradford Labour Institute in 1893, when over one-third of the 120 delegates had come from Yorkshire's woollen districts and they had debated such topics as the employment of children, the abolition of overtime and the care of the disabled. Horse-drawn Clarion Vans took Socialist speakers and propaganda about the manufacturing North; members of local ILP branches spent winter nights undergoing vigorous lecture-courses. A former Civil Service clerk from Cowling, Philip Snowden, emerged as a West Riding leader; dour, crippled and dedicated, his subject was 'The Religion of Socialism'. Under Socialist pressure, the Liberal government, during the decade before 1914, was induced to carry out a number of social measures which included the medical inspection of schoolchildren, the payment of National Insurance contributions, and the introduction of old age pensions. 'Well! Aw nivver knew nought like it!' a hardy Yorkshire 84-year-old greeted the latter in disbelief. 'They browt a looad o' coils afoor Kursmiss, an' now five shillin' i' t'week as long as Aw live! An' Aw've done nowt for nawther on 'em!'

Saddlers and harness-makers, blacksmiths and wheelwrights still enjoyed a plentiful employment, for the horse remained the

68   Chaff-cutting about the turn of the century

175

principal means of road transport; the mainstay of an agriculture depressed by two and a half decades of bad weather, sheep-rot and foot-and-mouth disease, the unequal competition of cheaper foreign commodities, and an exodus of farm workers off the land into the towns. Horses even, still, made possible the occasional treat by pulling the waggonette and the canal-barge of exuberant half-day trippers. Yet change was in the air. A bicycle craze pointed the way towards shrinking distances and the ability of a larger populace to travel under its own efforts. At the same time, as the first new-fangled 'motor-carists' appeared, public transport was being revolutionised as jogging horse-trams gave place to steam traction and electricity. Huddersfield Corporation, the first local authority to assume responsibility for steam trams in 1882, had run part of its Board of Trade inspection with the brake inadvertently on—not surprisingly' several unsatisfactory attempts' failed to move the car uphill! Nine years later, a line opened at Roundhay, Leeds, pioneered the use of the electric overhead wire. At Sheffield, which electrified its system a few years later, drivers were requested to sound their bells as little as possible when passing churches and chapels on Sundays.

The Great War changed everything. Indeed, Yorkshire received a shockingly symbolic baptism of twentieth-century fire late in 1914, when German cruisers shelled her east coast, selecting for an early-morning bombardment the towns of Whitby and Scarborough—which the German press, with a disregard both for reality and geography, described as 'the most important harbour on the east coast of England between the Humber and the Thames, protected by a mole and batteries'. A single hour demonstrated the vulnerability of features hitherto stable, and the fortuitousness of sudden death, as casual shells killed a magistrate in his bedroom, a postman delivering a letter, a family of four, a railwayman leading a horse, a coastguard in his signal station. Scarborough's pier lighthouse took a direct hit; her stolid Victorian hotels gaped open; the catalogue of damage included the Castle, the Town Hall, the Co-operative stores, the South Cliff gardens . . . even the ruins of Whitby Abbey fell, in the high-flown journalism of the period, 'a victim to the vindictive spite of an enemy'. At least, the 'atrocity' (the Scarborough inquest jury wanted to return a verdict of 'wilful murder') was good for recruiting. 'Men of Yorkshire,' one poster appealed, 'Show the Enemy that

Yorkshire will exact a full penalty for this Cowardly Slaughter Enlist Today'.

The Great War unleashed a patriotic fervour which brought men flocking to the colours, encouraged, in the earlier stages, by emotional and sometimes ingenuous recruiting posters. 'Yorkshire,' declaimed the 6th Reserve Battalion of the Duke of Wellington's Regiment, 'with its broad acres, dense population and strapping sons, must not lag behind in this life and death struggle against the German military despot.' In the Wolds, Sir Mark Sykes of Sledmere formed his tenants, accustomed to horses, into the Yorkshire Waggoners' Reserve and presented them to the Army Service Corps. A Bradford Pals' Battalion adopted the sporty slogan: 'Play the Game!' and appealed for the enlistment of 'dashing forwards' (Full-back: Lord Kitchener; Three-quarter backs: General French, Admiral Jellicoe, Lord Fisher and General Smith-Dorrien). A Leeds Pals' Battalion recruited 1,200 men within a few weeks. Drums and bugles of military bands stirred the blood; enthusiastic speeches filled halls and squares; illuminated tramcars blazed with exhortations—'Nah Then, John Willie, Ger Agate, Lad, an' Join t'Army'—and the Lord Mayor of Leeds went to a football match 'especially to plead the needs of the nation', and 'secured two hundred recruits'. Then, as the sense of adventure palled under the realities of modern warfare, conscription maintained the supply of men and horrible statistics recorded the cost: the 1,100 men of the original 1/4th West Riding Regiment had by 1917 been reduced by 'death, sickness, and captures' to 70 . . . 484 Huddersfield men died in 1916 alone . . . some 9,640 Leeds men lost their lives throughout the War; whilst 2,000 Bradfordians killed in the Somme offensive demonstrated the tactlessness of recruiting units from the same areas. Professor F. W. Moorman, of the University of Leeds, caught the mood in his dialect *Flowers of Knaresborough Forest*:

Ploo-lads frae Pannal have crossed ower the Channel,
Shipperds frae Fewston have taen the King's pay,
Thackrays frae Dacre have sold ivery acre;
Thou'll finnd ne'er a delver frae Haverah to Bray.

Taking men's places on the home front, women emerged to play that part in the working world which would win them the vote in 1918. In industrial Yorkshire, where female labour had supported the factory system for generations, this changing role came naturally to many, but new appeals were being made to 'women who do not usually do paid work'. So they became tram drivers and conductresses (not without early opposition and threats of men's strike action), railway cleaners and ticket collectors, postwomen and telegraph messengers, and filled the urgent employment demands of great new munitions works.

Yorkshire industry geared itself to war. National Shell Factories swung into operation in towns and cities: Leeds (which boasted a woman worker who could rifle an 18-pounder gun in two hours 40 minutes) produced a grand total of 1·5 m. shells, plus thousands of millions of fuses. 714,000 high-explosive shells manufactured in Keighley were sufficient, in the words of the chairman of the local War Munitions Committee, to have 'won the battle of Waterloo'. The most serious of three explosions at the Barnbow Ordnance factory killed 35 young women; in another, at the Low Moor chemical works, Bradford—a censored press simply called it 'a munitions factory in Yorkshire'—39 died, including six firemen. Laundry machine manufacturers switched to the production of field kitchens and disinfectors. Textile mills poured out miles of khaki and flannel, Leeds alone made 87 m. cartridge bags and 26 m. exploder bags. Even schoolchildren were set to work stitching sandbags.

Agriculture too expanded under the impetus of a submarine war which brought the threat—and occasionally the reality, though carefully underplayed by the newspapers—of food riots. 'We must all eat less food,' ran a typical circular from the Ministry of Food, 'especially we must all eat less bread and none of it must be wasted. The enemy is trying to take away our daily bread. He is sinking our wheat ships. If he succeeds in starving us our soldiers will have died in vain'. Children were showered with 'Mr Slice o' Bread' leaflets: 'I am a Slice of Bread. I measure three inches by two-and-a-half, and my thickness is half-an-inch. My weight is exactly an ounce. I am wasted once a day by 48,000,000 people of Britain . . . When you throw me away or waste me you are adding 20 submarines to the German Navy.' Accordingly, the Government initiated a ploughing-up movement, which came, however, like compulsory rationing, only towards the War's latter stages. The cultivation of allotments was strenuously

69 *Women munitions workers from a National Shell Factory at Keighley, posing on a fund-raising tableau in 1916*

encouraged; parks, sports fields and golf links went under oats, sprouted potatoes and cauliflowers and cabbages; classes went outdoors for lessons on wild edible greenstuffs, and housewives attended lectures and cookery demonstrations with titles like 'How to Provide Dinners at 4*d* to 6*d*.'

The Armistice of November, 1918, coinciding as it did with an influenza epidemic which throughout the world was killing an estimated 10 m., came almost as an anti-climax. Everywhere, in churches and chapels and cemeteries, communities poured their subscriptions into an eloquence of plaques, cenotaphs, statues, windows, institutes. The inscription on the Victory Medal, 'The Great War for Civilisation', and the peace celebrations which filled the streets with processions of Sunday School tableaux sporting titles like 'The Dawn of a New World', bright with angels, Britannias and John Bulls, were to prove sadly indicative of a wishful thinking. An apparent trade boom which followed the end of hostilities flashed in the pan, after all. The war had acted as a melting-pot: old social strata were crumbling, wages and prices disrupted, and industries had been artificially geared to wartime needs. Now Britain, crippled by war debts, failed to hold her own in world markets, and 1921 ushered in the trauma of slump. Coal, iron and steel production shrank; the importation of cheaper Empire food spelled ruin for agriculture; textile exports spectacularly dropped—more than half the work-force in Huddersfield lost their jobs within months—and unemployment became a drab fact of life. The savings of innumerable families disappeared in eking out the dole; formerly successful businessmen had recourse to the workhouse; pawnshops played a vital role; boys trundled home-made box-carts to tips and spent, one of them would recall, 'an hour or two scratting about amongst the filth and rubbish to find all the unburnt bits of coal and coke and cinders, as black as the hobs of Hell'.

A period of political and industrial unrest reached deadlock in the nine-day General Strike of May, 1926, disrupting transport and other industries, and forcing the *Yorkshire Observer*, due to the cessation of work by its technical staff—'without motive, and in flagrant disregard of their contracts of service'—to put out the news through a brief staccato series of duplicated strike bulletins. There was much indeed to report. At Leeds, the scene of repeated police baton charges, the few trams continuing to run were pelted with lumps of coal, and carried an escort of constables. A milk train was stoned at Shipley, and 200 York strikers tried to hold up a train at a level crossing. Four Sheffield men, presumably seething with revolutionary intent, were arrested whilst 'carrying a Lewis gun wrapped in brown paper' through the streets. Yet there was no wide-spread disorder—the militancy of many public transport strikers was tamely expended in jeering, to little avail, at the private buses and chars-a-banc which coolly took over their passengers. Volunteer tram and engine drivers, firemen and porters offered their services in their thousands, motorists displayed cards saying 'Signal for a Lift', and West Riding textile goods flowed fairly smoothly to Hull on lorries which made the

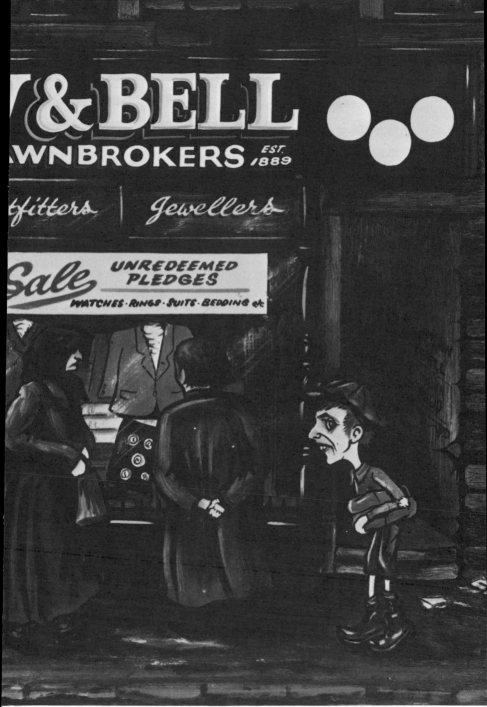

70   *The Pawnshop, from a painting by Stanley R. Boardman*

return journey laden with food-stuffs. Emergency food officers, on the whole, were able to assure few shortages, little panic buying, and 'the managers of the places of amusement report that the strike has not made any difference in the numbers of their audiences'.

This last was a significant consideration, for the between-the-wars era, escapist despite its difficulties, set considerable store by its entertainments. Provincial theatres, albeit making little attempt to stretch the intellect, regaled steady houses with programmes consisting primarily of revues, variety turns and musical comedies. The cinema had entered its heyday—'Book Your Seats', their advertising usually advised—and motion-picture dramas were always 'gripping', their adventures 'tremendous', and their comedies invariably 'screamingly funny'. Dancing and roller-skating were in vogue, sport had assumed its disproportionate role in the pattern of working-class life, and the pleasures of hiking and cycling and camping were being increasingly sampled. The motor char-a-banc had brought the outing within nearly everybody's reach, and day-trippers universally clad in cloth caps and big hats rode companionably six to a seat, at modest speeds beneath the open skies or doubtful shelter of the folding canvas hood, bouncing on solid tyres and putting their trust in a new breed of youngish men who had learnt their driving in Army lorries (Yorkshire claims the dubious distinction of the first serious char-a-banc accident, late in 1920, when the brakes failed in a Maudsley full of knur-and-spell supporters from Pecket Well; which ran out of control down Cockhill Moor and smashed through a wall above Oxenhope Church, killing five). And all the while, of course, the motor-bicycle and the motor-car were becoming ever the more ubiquitous.

An age which can perhaps be too glibly glimpsed in terms of stark depression on the one hand, or giddy gaiety on the other, witnessed nonetheless very substantial social advances. Slum clearance, begun in the 1920s, progressed with a kind of idealistic zeal during the following decade. 'New Homes for the People!' and 'Houses for Heroes to Live In!' became telling slogans in the promotion of the invariably 'sunny' estates of a new suburbia of highly desirable residences. 'All you need to do,' the glossy brochures assured the well-to-do, 'is consult your Architect or Builder, and choose a site'; whilst for their poorer citizens, local authorities instituted brave re-housing programmes. Leeds pioneered with its revolutionary 23-acre Quarry Hill Flats striving to achieve a sense of community, complete with their own shops, post office, playgrounds, lifts, an air-suction refuse system, and an incinerator designed to heat water for the communal laundry. If less inspired housing estates tended all too often to sprawl brashly across the landscape, they still represented a long step forward from their bug-ridden, back-to-back predecessors, though the transplanted tenant was sometimes nonplussed by his new luxury of a garden. What was perhaps more to the purpose, his wife was now acquiring access to a maternity clinic, his children were being given milk at school and the opportunity to attend a summer camp, and his meat came to his table, not by way of the poleaxe and some unhygienic back-street slaughter-house, but from a clean new abattoir.

The slow haul of economic recovery in pace with the development of fresh fields for industry was overshadowed, during the thirties, by the threat once more of conflict. Yorkshire's long coastline offered an obvious target for invasion from an enemy-occupied Europe, and the Humber featured strongly in between-the-wars defence schemes. In the event, Hull, within easy reach of German bomber crews, suffered repeated air attacks, countering in 1942 with the installation of a 'dazzle barrage' of massed searchlights. Sheffield, important in armaments and aircraft production—at the beginning of the War its English Steel Corporation was the country's sole manufacturer of Rolls-Royce Merlin crankshafts for fighter planes—was heavily raided in December of 1940, with more than 700 killed. York, too, became the predictable victim of a 'Baedeker' raid (targets were chosen for their historic appeal and lack of defences), clusters of incendiaries dropping both north and south of the Minster. Yet the necessities of meeting the demands of modern warfare brought a needed impetus alike to an industry and an agriculture increasingly subject to government supervision, as the county's resources and manpower were geared to the winning of the second world war in a generation.

The last three decades have accelerated earlier trends. The loss of empire markets, the growth of foreign competition and the rising costs of production have exercised a restrictive effect on the West Riding's traditional industries, its woollens and worsteds and coal; whilst mechanisation has replaced the heavy manual labour of iron and steel with a high degree of sophistication. Mechanisation also has transformed Yorkshire's agriculture: its East and North Riding farms are larger, fewer and more efficient than heretofore, though a proportion of its smaller Pennine homesteads crumble back into their hard moors. Advanced education lies now within easier reach; to the universities of Leeds and Sheffield, respectively of late Victorian and Edwardian foundation, have been added those of Bradford, Hull and York, to say nothing of a host of polytechnics and training colleges. The decline of religion has occasioned a monumental demolition of churches and chapels and Sunday Schools, or their conversion into flats and warehouses. The residences of Victorian mill magnates do duty now as offices or museums, as schools or nursing homes.

The implementation of the Local Government Act of 1972 has ended the traditional administrative geography of the county itself, creating new counties of North, West and South Yorkshire. Part of the former East Riding has joined a slice of Lincolnshire to form a county of Humberside; part of the North Riding, Teesside and County Durham have become the county of Cleveland; Sedbergh has been lost to Cumbria. The old Ridings apportioned by the Vikings have ceased to exist. . . .

FURTHER READING

Chapter 9
Frederick Alderson: *View North: A Long Look at Northern England*, 1968.
Mary Cathcart Borer: *Britain—Twentieth Century: The Story of Social Conditions*, 1966.
Basil Collier: 'The Defence of the United Kingdom' *(History of the Second World War: United Kingdom Military Series)*, 1957.
J. J. Fisher: *History of the Duke of Wellington's West Riding Regiment (the Iron Duke's Own) During the First Three Years of the Great War*, 1917.
W. Harwood Long, M.A.: *A Survey of the Agriculture of Yorkshire* (Royal Agricultural Society of England: County Agricultural Surveys, No. 6), 1969.
Henry Pelling: *The Origins of the Labour Party, 1880–1900*, 1965.

B. Seebohm Rowntree and May Kendall: *How the Labourer Lives: A Study of the Rural Labour Problem*, 1913.

B. Seebohm Rowntree: *Poverty: a Study of Town Life*, 1901.

William Herbert Scott: *Leeds in the Great War, 1914–1918*, 1923.

John J. Waddington-Feather: *Leeds: the Heart of Yorkshire*, 1967.

Andrew D. Young: *One Hundred Years of Leeds Tramways*, 1970.

Index

Heywood, Rev. Oliver, 81–2
Holden, Isaac, 155
Hospitals, 49–50, 88
Housing, 145, 182–3
Huddersfield, 125, 146, 176
Hudson, George, 144
Hull, 67, 72, 93, 134, 162, 183

Ice Age, 11
Ilkley, 17, 155
Improvement Commissioners, 150–1
Ingham, Benjamin, 110
Ingleborough, 17
Iron Age, 14
Iron and steel, 67, 121–2, 135

Jacobite Rebellion, 107
James the Deacon, 28
Jefferys, Thomas, 102
Jessop, Arthur, 107
Jews, 45
Jutes, 26

Kay, John, 119
Keighley, 22, 48, 123, 145
Kent, William, 111
Kirkdale Cave, 11
Kitson, John, 126

Labour Party, 173
Lambert, John, 77
Leeds, 66, 95, 96, 114, 146, 150, 183
Leeds Town Hall, 153
Libraries, 110–1
Locomotive engines, 133–4
Luddites, 124–6

Malton, 20, 24
Manors, 38–9, 68
Maps, 101–2
Markets, 48–9, 95
Marshall, John, 121, 136, 158
Marshall, William, 103
Marston Moor, Battle of, 75
Marvell, Andrew, 86
Masborough Ironworks, 122
Meaux Abbey, 50
Mechanics' Institutes, 157–9
Meriton, George, 86–7
Metcalf, John, 97
Methodism, 108–10
Micklegate Bar, 55–6, 107
Middleham Castle, 57
Middlesbrough, 135
Middleton Colliery, 133–4
Monasteries, 29, 45–8, 59
Monasteries, Dissolution of, 59–63
Moravians, 110
Mother Shipton, 84
Municipal Corporations Act, 151
Munitions, 178
Mystery Plays, 50–2
Myton, Battle of, 45

National Society for Promoting the Education
  of the Poor in the Principles of the
  Established Church, 159–60
Navvies, 100, 143–4

Newspapers, 110, 167
New Stone Age, 16
Nonconformism, 108–10, 163–4
Northallerton, 92
Northallerton, Battle of, 45
Northumbria, Kingdom of, 27–31

Oastler, Richard, 132
Ogilby, John, 101
Oswald, 28
Oswin, 28
Oswy, 28
Owen, Robert, 162–3

Parisi, 20
Parks, 165
Parliamentary representation, 113–4, 135–6
Pateley Bridge, 146
Paulinus, 27
Peasants, 39, 50
Penda, 28
Pilgrimage of Grace, 60–1, 68
Place-names, 32
Plagues, 50, 71, 79
Plug Riots, 137
Pontefract Castle, 76
Poor Law Amendment Act, 138
Poor relief, 114–6, 138
Population, 123, 172
Powell, Foster, 108
Preston, Benjamin, 168–9
Priestley, Joseph, 113
Priestley, Thomas, 80
Printing, 59
Punishments, 33, 66, 82–4

Quakers, 85–6, 107
Quarry Hill Flats, 183

Railways, 142–4
Recusancy, 65
Reform Act, 136
Resurrection-men, 108
Richard III, 57
Richmond, 44, 92, 111
Ridings, 33, 123, 184
Rievaulx Abbey, 42
Riots, 96, 114, 124–6, 137
Ripon, 29, 49–50
Rising of the North, 64–5
Roads, 19, 87–8, 95
Robin Hood, 39
Rolle, Richard, 50
Romans, 16–24
Rombalds Moor, 14
Rowntree, Benjamin Seebohm, 172–3
Rupert, Prince, 75

Sadler, Michael Thomas, 127, 132, 136
St. George's Hall, Bradford, 151
Salt, Sir Titus, 135, 153–5
Saltaire, 153–5
Saxons, 26
Saxton, Christopher, 70
Scarborough, 14, 24, 89, 106–7, 155, 176–9
Scarborough Castle, 63, 76
Schools, 59, 86, 159–60
Scoresby, William, 112